the race
run like a champion

SAMMY TIPPIT

Ambassador International
GREENVILLE, SOUTH CAROLINA & BELFAST, NORTHERN IRELAND

www.ambassador-international.com

the race
run like a champion

Printed in the United States of America

ISBN: 978-1-935507-50-5

Cover Design by David Siglin of A&E Media

Page Layout by Kelley Moore of Points & Picas

AMBASSADOR INTERNATIONAL
Emerald House
427 Wade Hampton Blvd.
Greenville, SC 29609, USA
www.ambassador-international.com

AMBASSADOR BOOKS
The Mount
2 Woodstock Link
Belfast, BT6 8DD, Northern Ireland, UK
www.ambassador-international.com

The colophon is a trademark of Ambassador

Dedication

To: Coach "Boots" Garland who has been one of the great speed coaches in America and a true friend during this past year.

To: Dr. Dennis Kinlaw, former President of Asbury College, a man who has inspired me as I've watched him run *The Race*.

In Memory

Dr. Bobby Moore, who ran well and finished his race—he left an example of how to run *The Race* that God has given each of us.

I never fail to come away inspired after hearing or reading something from Sammy Tippit. *The Race* is no exception. You'll be challenged and refreshed if you let its message reach your soul.
—JERRY B. JENKINS
Co-Author of the *Left Behind* series
Colorado Springs, Colorado

I was gripped from the first word of *The Race*! If you are a sports fan, a God fan, or just a fan of living the life you were meant to live, you are going to love this book. Even better, you will be changed by it. You will run!
—DR. JOHN AVANT
Senior Pastor
First Baptist Church, West Monroe, Louisiana

As a runner throughout my life and as one who has competed in the Boston Marathon, I have been enthralled with the stories and life lessons in The Race. As a friend of and fellow minister with Sammy Tippit for over thirty years, I know the heart of this champion for the gospel of Jesus and the price he has paid to proclaim it. And, like Sammy, I know that champions, in both running and life, become champions because they face and overcome adversity. The athletic insights in The Race will help you turn life's painful experiences into awesome victories, and they will cause you to run life's daily race with a more intense focus on The Finish Line!
—BARRY ST.CLAIR,
President,
Reach Out Youth Solutions, Atlanta, GA

Sammy Tippit lives what he writes about. I've been blessed to hear him share his heart on this subject and to now see it in print is a double blessing. Sammy is one who has run the race well. He is a champion on every level. *The Race* is a book you will want to read and recommend to others.
—MICHAEL CATT
Senior Pastor
Sherwood Church, Albany, Georgia
Executive Producer, Sherwood Pictures

contents

What an incredible challenge! I just couldn't put it down! In a day of lukewarmness and half-heartedness, *The Race* challenged me to a higher level of personal discipline. Sammy has done it again! Another book that pours his journey into mine.

—DAVE ENGBRECHT
Senior Pastor

Nappanee Missionary Church, Nappanee, IndianaSammy Tippit brings together his experiences as a runner along with the wealth of biblical material that applies to running and physical fitness, and gives us a challenging word for running the Christian life in a way that honors Christ. I was rebuked, encouraged, and trained as I read, and feel better equipped to run the race before me.

—DAVE BUTTS
Chairman
America's National Prayer Committee

Embedded within these pages lie some critical forgotten factors that will help ignite a fire for personal revival while enabling you to endure the challenges we all experience on our journey toward Christ-likeness. Discover and digest these truths, and the times of refreshing God wants you to experience will enable you to complete life's race successfully.

—BYRON PAULUS
Executive Director
Life Action Ministries

The Race is the perfect example of a dramatic human plot portrayed before divine themes that are as real to the reader as the pages upon which they are written. A masterpiece! You can't put this one down!

—DR. JOE AGUILLARD
President
Louisiana College, Pineville, Louisiana

foreword

I first met Sammy Tippit a little over thirty years ago when he was inspiring a generation of young people across America. He continues to motivate people today to fulfill their potential in life. He presents us with an incredible challenge in his latest book, *The Race*. I readily understood the pain, agony, and victory in his story of running the course of the original Greek marathon.

While Governor of Arkansas, I quit digging my grave with a knife and fork and took up running and lost more than 100 pounds, and completed 4 marathons. Since then, I've realized there is a great health crisis in America. As a people, we need the inspiration, motivation, and discipline to make lifestyle choices that place us on the road towards health.

Sammy Tippit provides such inspiration and motivation in *The Race*. His story of his bout with cancer and decision to run the original Greek marathon shows the way to overcoming life's great adversities. It's laced with testimonies from some of America's great athletes. Yet, this book is much more than a tutorial on running. It's about life and how an ordinary person can live as a champion.

Sammy Tippit intertwines running principles with biblical truths that show the way to personal renewal, strength and character development. Reading his words and sensing his excitement, you will want to run well *The Race*. He provides practical insights to running and living from men like Ryan Hall,

America's great marathoner. The book is deeply spiritual, very practical, and extremely helpful.

It's filled with exciting stories and life lessons that will enable you to run *The Race* and run it well.

—GOVERNOR MIKE HUCKABEE

acknowledgements

Several runners and coaches have helped me to understand the running principles found in this book. Many thanks to Ryan Hall, America's great marathoner. He opened his heart and understanding about endurance running as well as *The Race*. Charles Austin, Olympic and American record holder, spent time helping me to understand how to overcome injuries. Former L.S.U. head football coach, Jerry Stovall, taught me the meaning of focus and discipline. My former high school track coach and former L.S.U. track coach, "Boots" Garland, reintroduced me to the basics of speed training. Julio Reyes taught me the value of running hills, and Tom Flournoy has been a great running partner. Kirsta Leeburg Melton ran the *Athens Classic Marathon* with me. I appreciate all of their input into my life and understanding of these running truths.

Others challenged me to bring this manuscript to a higher level. Les Stobbe challenged me to think outside the box and write with greater creativity. Andy Scheer did wonders with editing the manuscript. It's been a privilege to work with the publishing team at Ambassador International. My wife, Tex, has been my best critic and a pro at proof reading the manuscript.

Running is basically an individual sport, but this book has been a team effort. I couldn't have done it without the team.

introduction

rejoice, we conquer!

Nenikékamen!
Pheidippides, 490 B.C.

… In all these things we have complete victory through him who loved us!
Romans 8:37

Plains of Marathon, Greece, 490 B.C.

Bodies littered the marsh surrounding the Athenian warrior. Sweat dripped from his face and onto the dead Persian soldier. Pheidippides pulled his sword out of the Persian, pointed it heavenward, and shouted, "Nenikékamen! (Rejoice, we conquer!)"

Thousands of Athenians responded, "Nenikékamen!"

Then silence. Everyone stood in awe, watching the Persian ships pull out of the bay.

➡ ➡ ➡ ➡ ➡ ➡

Behind the troops, generals laughed, shouted, and slapped each other on the back, congratulating one another on their victory.

General Miltiades didn't participate in the celebration but watched the fleeing ships. "Gentlemen, don't celebrate too quickly," he said. "A few thousand of us chased 80,000 barbarians into the sea, but that doesn't mean the battle is over. I assure you that Darius's warriors aren't through. Those ships are not headed back to Persia. They are sailing for Athens. The city is without protection."

General Aristides' smile fell. "What can we do?"

"Our troops must be in Athens within twenty-four hours," Miltiades said. "Meanwhile, we need to send a runner to announce the victory and let the people know we're coming." Miltiades' voice began trembling. "If we lose Athens, we will be slaves to the Persians. Civilization, as we know it, will no longer exist. Our freedoms, families, and future will be determined in the next twenty-four hours. We need a runner who can be there before the sun goes down."

Aristides replied with a caustic laugh. "For that, you need a man with wings of an eagle. That person doesn't exist."

Callimachus, the senior commander, interrupted. "I know a man with such wings."

➡ ➡ ➡ ➡ ➡ ➡

"Pheidippides, come quickly. The generals need you!" a soldier shouted as he ran toward the exhausted warrior. "They said it's urgent."

Pheidippides turned, smiled at his fellow soldiers, then did what he did best—run. Exhausted but exhilarated, the well-toned athlete seemed not to feel any effects of the blistering heat and the bloody battle. Adrenaline ran through his veins as joy flooded his emotions.

As Pheidippides entered the generals' tent, he scanned the contrasting environment. No blood, no sweat—just brilliant minds and fancy battle gear.

As the young athlete approached Miltiades and Aristides, they scanned his body. "So you're the one who runs faster than the chariots," Miltiades said. "And today, you chased the barbarians back into the sea where they belong."

"*We*, sir. *We* chased them back. With your leadership and our men's courage, we were destined to win."

"You're right, Pheidippides. But the battle isn't over," Aristides said. "The barbarians will attack Athens. We need a runner to announce our victory. Athenians must prepare food and water for our arrival. You are the fastest and best runner we have. You need to be there before the sun goes down. That will give them ample opportunity to prepare."

Pheidippides nodded. "I am honored and at your disposal."

"Are you sure you can be there before nightfall?" Miltiades said. "You fought today with all of the intensity any human could muster. Do you have the endurance to run twenty-six miles—half of it up hills?"

Pheidippides' face exuded confidence.

"Sir," he said. "You are a professional. Your leadership made the Persians flee like cowards. I, too, am a professional. Trust me. I can be in Athens in less than four hours. All Athenians will rejoice and be ready to receive the troops. I will run with fire in my heart and the wind at my back."

Miltiades put his hand on Pheidippides' shoulder. "Then clean your shoes. While you do that, we will gather water and food for you. Then you must go quickly."

Aristides spoke gently to the young athlete. "Be careful. The sun is hotter than normal. It can be deadly."

"Sir, the heat, the wind—nothing will stop me. Before the sun goes down, I promise you I will announce the victory." Pheidippides laid down his shield, cleaned his shoes, ate a quick bite, and began running.

The first mile was filled with soldiers cheering, "Nenikékamen!" His adrenaline ran so high, he started too fast. Once he passed the crowds, Pheidippides was at home. Thoughts of the battle filled his mind. The lonely runner. A man with a mission. This time he wasn't running to beat the competition but for the glory and safety of all Athenians. That goal was much higher than any of the competitions in which he had ever participated.

After two miles, Pheidippides relaxed and began talking to himself. "Take it easy. Slow it down. You still have a long way to go."

The breeze coming from the sea refreshed his body and renewed his mind. He felt like he had so many times before as he fell into his pace. His arms and legs moved with the rhythm of a professional dancer. As he glided down the road, he wondered what it would be like when he arrived in Athens. How would the people respond to the news of the victory?

At six miles, he felt strong. He needed only to run his race and stay on pace. At this point, he faced his first hill. It wasn't too bad. But he knew it was merely a shadow of what lay ahead. Once he was over the first hill, he smiled. *I'll conquer these hills just as we conquered the Persians.* He was getting into the zone.

When Pheidippides reached the halfway mark, he became certain he would reach Athens before the sun went down. His legs felt strong. His breathing remained level. He began climbing the hills. They weren't very steep—just long. He could see what appeared to be the top of a hill. But once he arrived there, the road took a turn and the hill just kept going. With the exception of a few short, flat areas, the hills ran continuously for almost ten miles.

Pheidippides knew exactly what to do: shorten his stride, slow his pace, and keep going.

His training seemed to pay off. He felt the impact of the ferocious battle, but his confidence remained high. He envisioned his entrance into Athens: children throwing flowers on the street, women cheering as he waved to the crowds, and the city elders congratulating him.

A secret, however, lurched inside his body. The heat was scorching, and the battle before this twenty-six miler had caused him to lose much water. He hadn't had time to replenish it. Some small warning signals began flashing. His skin dried out, his lips stuck to his gums, and his mouth felt stuffed with cotton. He was so well trained, however, that he paid no attention to the signs. Managing pain was part of his profession.

When Pheidippides reached mile twenty, he was on top of the hills. *I've run them the way they should have been run. I've done it. The rest will be easy. It's all downhill now.*

But during the next mile, everything began to fall apart. *Where did that come from? Why are my hips becoming stiff?* Pain shot through one hip, then the other. He realized he needed water and food. Yet he still had six more miles before he reached the city. *It's not that far. I can make it,* he told himself. *Then I will be re-freshed.* The dirty little secret, *dehydration,* began to expose itself.

Pheidippides hadn't felt that kind of pain since he first started running. Though he was going downhill, his pace slowed considerably. The pain spread as he felt cramping in his quads. Then his calves. With just a couple of miles left, Pheidippides couldn't run any farther. He began walking. Every time his foot struck the ground, it felt like someone lit a fire on his soles. He was a strong, tough runner—but nothing ever hurt like this. His legs trembled. He staggered and looked like a drunkard coming into Athens. It wasn't what he had dreamed.

As he entered the city, no one was sure what Pheidippides was doing. Most thought he was drunk. They stared and laughed. Athens's greatest athlete couldn't control his legs. No one understood.

The cramping in his legs grew stronger. His head felt like someone was battering it with a sledge hammer. His mind played tricks as he bent over in exhaustion. He saw that blood filled his shirt. *Could I have been wounded in the battle and not known it?* He lifted his shirt and saw his nipples bleeding. He ripped off his shirt, taking the scab with it, screaming in agony.

He fell to his knees. *I have to finish. I must make it to the elders and announce the victory.* He could go no farther.

Finally he lifted himself off the ground and stood still while the world around him seemed to spin. *I'm going to faint. I must start running.* But he couldn't. Frozen in pain, the athlete tried to regain his strength. But nothing was there. He then felt his life leaving him. "No," he whispered. "I can't die now."

Pheidippides looked up, focused on the road ahead, and began running.

The crowds began cheering. Nothing could stop the young athlete now. People ran out of their homes and shouted encouragement as he ran into the city's center. The elders were waiting. One walked up to Pheidippides and waited for him to speak. The crowds gathered around him.

Pheidippides bent over with his head hanging down. It seemed like an eternity before he looked up.

His eyes glazed over. He attempted to speak, but couldn't.

Several men gathered around him and took his hands off his knees and helped him to stand. He looked at the crowd. Children showered him with flowers. Women cheered. The elders waited. It was no dream. With all the strength he could gather, Pheidippides shouted with a whisper, "Nenikékamen!"

Then he collapsed and died.

2500 Years Later

(Email sent from Athens, Greece, on November 2, 2008)

Greetings from Sammy (almost Pheidippides) Tippit!

You'll need to read the end of this email to understand the Pheidippides part and what took place at the end of the race. When the original Olympic committee decided to have a distance race in 1896, they determined to use the course of Pheidippides. Consequently, the race was called *marathon* because of the victory won by the Greeks on the plains of Marathon.

Now what does that have to do with me? Many of you are aware that when I was diagnosed with cancer, God put it on my heart to run this original marathon course. Ken Leeburg, my best friend from 30 years ago, and I had dreamed about running it. Then Ken was killed in an automobile accident, and the dream was lost—until the cancer diagnosis.

Ken's oldest daughter, Kirsta Leeburg Melton, felt she wanted to run with me in place of her dad. She came to Greece with Ken's name inscribed on her bib and a photo of her dad in a small picture frame she carried with her.

This morning, Kirsta's husband, Wade, accompanied Kirsta and me to that original Olympic stadium to catch a bus to the starting line in the village of Marathon. (My wife, Tex, became ill, and I had to call a doctor to come treat her as I left the hotel.)

The race started promptly at 9:00 a.m., and I was off to a good start. I didn't see Kirsta until later at the stadium—that's where the story gets interesting.

I ran the first three miles at an 8:42 per mile pace, which was great for me. It felt easy. That pace would have put me well under 4 hours, which I was hoping to accomplish. I kept the same pace through six miles and felt strong. Between six and twelve miles, there were a number of hills, but my time remained fairly consistent. I dropped to about an 8:50 pace. But I was still on pace to run a sub-four-hour marathon.

Everything between twelve and twenty miles was hills—*big hills, long hills. Terrible hills!* I knew I was far enough ahead of my schedule that I could slow my pace until the top of the hills and still finish under four hours. The final 6.2 miles were either downhill or flat. I figured I could handle it.

But when I completed the hills, I was completely exhausted. My goal was to make it to the refreshment station about a mile away. I made it, took a drink, then walked a good way. When I tried to run, everything in my body hurt!

At first, my goal was to be able to jog slowly to the next refreshment station, rehydrate, and walk some more. But that proved too difficult. The pain increased with every step.

I decided I would try to jog to the next distance marker and then walk. I made it but didn't think I could go any farther.

I then tried to make it to the next red light. I succeeded but was so fatigued, I could hardly move. I began walking and then jogging. After a while, I hurt so badly I didn't think I would even be able to walk.

I was doing this for the glory of God—and the memory of my dear friend, Ken Leeburg. I knew I couldn't quit. But it was *so* hard. At a half mile from the finish, I hurt so badly, I wept.

As I was ready to give up, I turned a corner to the street that led directly to the Olympic stadium. It's hard to describe the scene. Hundreds of people lined the street, shouting, "Bravo, Bravo!"

I wept, looked unto the Lord, and His strength rose within me. I began jogging. People kept shouting! As I arrived at the stadium, the scene was incredible. That first Olympic stadium was filled with thousands of people shouting, "Bravo, Bravo!"

I ran down the straightaway to the cheering crowds of this historic stadium with my finger pointing toward heaven—hurting so badly and weeping with deep emotion.

Sammy at the 13.1 kilometer mark in the *Athens Classic Marathon.*

As I crossed the finish line, all I could say was, "I did it. I finished the race." But I quickly became disoriented, and the man in charge of our running tour saw me, knew something was wrong, and brought me water.

Johnathan Macris, a Greek friend, was filming me. He ran up with the video camera and asked for a comment.

"This was the most difficult thing I have ever done in my life," I said. "I didn't run as fast as I hoped. But I decided that speed was not the most important thing, but finishing the race was what mattered."

Then I said, "I feel like I'm going to faint."

The sky started spinning, and everything became fuzzy. Paramedics rushed over and grabbed me as I collapsed. I don't remember the next few minutes, except that I was put on a stretcher and brought to the medical tent. Several doctors worked on me. I felt lifeless as I lay there.

I remained in the medical tent for a couple hours. Kirsta crossed the finish line one hour after me. Johnathan's son, Justin, told her where I was. Meanwhile, the doctors decided I needed to go to the hospital.

As I was transported to the hospital, the paramedic in the ambulance asked Johnathan about my running and who I was.

He shared my story—and the gospel—with her. At the hospital, I went through a battery of tests—blood tests, EKG, x-Rays, and physical exams by cardiologists and internal medicine doctors.

The physicians asked, "Is this your first marathon?"

I said yes. Then they asked, "How old are you?"

When I told them I was 61, they began speaking very quickly in Greek. I later learned that I was the second man that day to have the same thing happen to him. It was his first marathon, and he was 60 years old. The difference between us was that he died.

Finally, the doctors released me, and I am now safely in my hotel room with my sweet wife. I am back to normal, and you don't need to worry about us. We will be okay. We would appreciate your prayers. We fly to Amsterdam tomorrow, where we will spend the night. We then leave the next day for 10 days of ministry in India.

Please pray that God would complete His healing in Tex and give us strength to continue. We appreciate you.

Sammy and Tex Tippit

THE RACE

Welcome to *The Race*. Two stories—so different, yet similar. One became the inspiration for the other. One is rooted in Greek tradition, the other in fact and biblical conviction. Both are filled with seeming contradictions. Some historians doubt the authenticity of Pheidippides running from the plains of Marathon to Athens to announce the Greeks' victory. Yet the original international Olympic committee believed it and made it the long-distance race of the first modern Olympic Games. Since then, the race has been called the *marathon*.

Both stories serve as the basis for *The Race*. This book is about life principles learned from the biblical imagery of the athlete, especially the runner. It contains testimonies of some of the world's greatest sports figures—their successes and failures, triumphs and tragedies, the pain suffered and the lessons learned.

These truths will send a refreshing from heaven as you read the Bible through the eyes of a runner. They will place you on the path of success as you pursue your life's purpose. But most important, you'll understand what it takes to run the race of life and finish well. "Nenikékamen!" Rejoice, we conquer!

the preparation

a call to run

I want you to do more than just watch a race. I want you to take part in it. I want to compare faith to running in a race. It's hard. It requires concentration of will, energy of soul. You experience elation when the winner breaks the tape.... Maybe you haven't got a job. So who am I to say, "Believe, have faith," in the face of life's realities? I would like to give you something more permanent, but I can only point the way. I have no formula for winning the race. Everyone runs in her own way, or his own way. And where does the power come from, to see the race to its end? From within. Jesus said, "Behold, the Kingdom of God is within you."

Eric Liddell in the movie *Chariots of Fire*

Therefore, since we are surrounded by such a great cloud of witnesses, we must get rid of every weight and the sin that clings so closely, and run with endurance the race set out for us.

Hebrews 12:1

If it feels strange to read a book about running that's written by a 63-year-old cancer survivor, you're not alone. It feels even more bizarre to write it. I would never have attempted it except that I've seen thousands of people helped in the past few years by these truths—and the renewal God brought to my life.

When I was in my early twenties, I experienced a great spiritual renewal. My ministry was launched in an unusual manner when God spoke to my heart and told me to *walk*. That's right—*walk*. A group of seven of us trekked across America pushing a wheelbarrow loaded with Bibles. As we gave people Bibles, God gave us a glimpse of revival in America. We issued a call for Christians to seek God's face for a move of His Spirit in the land. Thousands of young people came to Christ as we watched a new generation of hot-hearted believers emerge.

God has now worked in a deeper and broader way than I experienced forty years ago. This time, He spoke to my heart: *Run*. If I had called the shots, I would have said *run* when I was young and *walk* when I was old. But God's ways are not our ways.

His ways are so much higher. There are truths in His Word that can spark a mighty revival in our land and renew our spiritual passion. These truths are profound but often missed by the casual reader. They enable us to not only begin well the race to which God has called us, but also finish well.

THE ATHLETE IN THE BIBLE

When Paul wrote to young Timothy, he used athletic terminology. He told Timothy, "If anyone competes as an athlete, he will not be crowned as the winner unless he competes according to the rules." A few phrases later he says, "Think about what I am saying and the Lord will give you understanding of all this" (2 Timothy 2:5, 7). Paul knew Timothy would understand such terminology because he grew up with a Greek father, and the athletic games were familiar to the Greeks. That terminology contains the secret to successful Christian living.

God wants us to finish life's race as winners, not losers. He longs to award us the crown of victory at the end of our lives. If you want to understand what that means, you must understand the athlete. You don't have to be an athlete to be a great Christian, but understanding the principles an athlete practices will enable you to live as "more than [a conqueror]" (Romans 8:37 ESV).

Paul also wrote, "With such affection for you we were happy to share with you not only the gospel of God but also our own lives, because you had become dear to us" (1 Thessalonians 2:8). Paul's love for them drove him not only to teach them biblical truths but also to impart his life experiences. It's with that heart that I write this book.

We now have more knowledge of the Bible in the Western world than at perhaps any other time in history. In the denomination to which I belong, more than two million sermons are preached every year from the Bible. When you multiply that by all the churches in various denominations, there are tens of millions of sermons preached annually in America. That doesn't include the sermons preached on radio, television, and the Internet. Yet all that information has had very little impact on today's culture.

We have much information but little understanding of the truth. We fill our notebooks, but our lives remain empty. We're strong on knowledge but weak on application. That may be one reason Jesus spoke in parables. They paint a picture of the truth that is plain and understandable. Once those truths are understood, the application becomes obvious.

When Paul wanted to pass the torch to Timothy, he used three types of imagery: the farmer, the soldier, and the athlete. He knew young Timothy would understand what he was saying and that all three of those images would challenge him to apply the truth—not just know it.

This book is filled with biblical truth and life stories, many of them my own, as well as lessons from some of the world's finest athletes. It is my heart's desire to not only impart the Word of God but also apply it.

God spoke to me through the metaphor of the athlete when He called me to run. It was the most practical call He's ever placed on my life. It not only brought a deep and lasting spiritual renewal, but it also showed me how to apply scriptural truths I've known for many years. It replaced head knowledge with practicing the truth.

These truths reach far beyond my experience on running trails. They transform anyone willing to embrace them. They hold the potential to make the reader a champion. The stories of Ryan Hall, American record-holder for the half marathon, and Charles Austin, the Olympic and American record-holder for the high jump, are incredible. They cause a profound faith to rise within us as we understand the powerful impact of the athletic metaphor.

These truths set you on a path that will enable you to fulfill your purpose by becoming more like Jesus. They lead you through suffering and make you a better person. They teach you how to turn weaknesses into strengths—and failure into victory. They enable you to run your race to your full potential.

It would seem to make more sense for a young man to write about the convergence of biblical truths with athletic principles. Yet I don't write these insights from what I learned as an athlete while in school. Instead I write from 45 years as a Christian—and as an athlete only the past few years.

THE JOURNEY

I was involved in athletics in high school. By the tenth grade, I had a case filled with trophies, from "Most Valuable Football Player" to "Most Valuable Basketball Player." I ran track in the tenth grade under "Boots" Garland, who later coached for LSU.

But I never capitalized on my talent. The problem was my lifestyle. Heavy drinking and smoking, in addition to asthma, cut short my athletic career. Over the years I've wondered what I might have accomplished had I addressed those issues.

While I was at LSU, Jesus became more than a historical figure to me. I believed in God—but had no personal relationship with Him. One night at Istrouma Baptist Church in Baton Rouge, a man spoke about knowing God in a very personal way. That man didn't have educational opportunities or a family that cared about him. Yet he had peace in his heart, a purpose in his life, and the attitude of a champion. I longed for those.

I prayed and invited Jesus to live within me—and I've never been the same. I walked into that church one person and walked out completely different. I entered a race in life that has continued until this day. A friend said, "Sammy, I'll give you two weeks, and you'll be back to the same old lifestyle." It's now been forty-five years, and I love Jesus more than ever.

Often people make a commitment to Christ, but the fire burning in their hearts gets dampened and they stop growing in their love for Jesus. I've seen many begin well but finish their race far below their potential. Some of my greatest heartbreaks have come from watching people who truly love God fall short of their potential.

Early in my ministry, I watched a fifteen-year-old high school student set his campus ablaze for God. He surrendered his life to the ministry and would often preach at youth meetings where 200 to 300 students gave their lives to Christ. He had as much potential as any other young man I've ever met. But a few years later most of that potential was lost when he left his wife for another woman. My heart breaks today knowing how God could have used him.

Yet failure isn't what keeps us from fulfilling our potential. Who hasn't failed? If a person learns from failure and makes the proper changes, he can heal from that injury. In a later chapter, we'll see how Charles Austin injured himself because of an improper technique but later became the world's greatest high jumper. He learned how to overcome his mistake, enabling him to achieve more than anyone thought possible.

Too many believers have fallen and never gotten back up. The greatest opportunities come to those who continue the process of developing Christlike character. One of my greatest longings is to help Christians run their life's race with endurance. To make that a reality, there must be seasons of refreshing throughout the journey. In most marathons, refreshment tables are located in strategic places along the course. Wise runners make sure they replenish themselves with water and necessary nutrients.

We often try to make key life decisions when we're exhausted. Instead of drinking from the fountain God has provided, we attempt to run life's race without being renewed. Consequently, God's race becomes a rat race. Spiritual dehydration results, and fatigue sets in. We finish far below our potential.

Three years after I entered into a personal relationship with Christ, I met a beautiful young lady with the nickname Tex. Soon, she and I were married. I told her, "I can't promise you we will ever be rich, but I do promise that life won't be boring." It hasn't. To share the good news of God's love, we've walked into the middle of a revolution in Romania, the aftermath of genocide in Rwanda, the middle of war zones in Burundi and Congo, and gang hangouts in Chicago.

We've climbed high mountains and tramped through deep valleys. We discovered great happiness on the mountaintops and developed Christian character in the valleys. Through it all, God has taught us incredible lessons. We learned most of them when we decided to travel down trails that led us to minister to hurting hearts.

A few years ago, however, the course of life took us a different direction from anything I ever imagined. Pain-filled tragedies tumbled us down mountains. The avalanche seemed never-ending. First, a dear friend was killed in an auto accident. Within weeks, I was hospitalized twice. Soon after that, a colleague was kidnapped by terrorists and brutally murdered.

Three weeks later, an unknown man from Portugal contacted me, saying he had evidence that he was my brother. One year later, I was diagnosed with cancer.

Instead of destroying my wife and me, this avalanche of difficulties made us stronger—and taught us how to live as champions.

In the middle of these catastrophes, I heard the still, small voice saying, *Run.* It sounded crazy. I didn't realize it at that moment, but my cancer diagnosis and that still, small voice would produce a great spiritual renewal in my soul—and may have extended my life.

As I attempted to obey that voice, I felt as though I was running through a field covered with gemstones and laced with gold. Each stone contained a truth from the Bible. I somehow knew I could find healing for my hurting heart and revival for my soul in those gems. As I picked them up, I not only grew stronger and healthier physically, I also became wealthy in a deeply spiritual way.

The farther I ran, the more plentiful and beautiful these gems became. I realized a goldmine must be nearby. I discovered it in a passage in one of the great books of the Bible: Hebrews. One verse gripped my heart. It set me on the road to personal renewal and has kept me on the path of a passionate pursuit of God's purpose.

THE ENDURANCE RACE

The author of Hebrews wrote, "We must ... run with endurance the race set out for us" (Hebrews 12:1). He compared the Christian life to running a particular kind of race—an endurance race.

Chapter 12 of Hebrews not only speaks of an endurance race in verse 1, but in verses 5 to 11 it also uses the word *discipline* eight times. Every athlete understands the necessity and meaning of discipline. Though this chapter of Hebrews speaks of discipline in the context of a father-son relationship, it follows the exhortation to run with endurance. In verse 11, we learn that discipline is a part of our "training." The passage then encourages the reader to "lift your drooping hands" and to "strengthen your weak knees" (v. 12 ESV). Both phrases continue the imagery of an athlete. This chapter then speaks of the

Sammy places second in his age division in *Baton Rouge Beach Half Marathon* just three months after doctor released him to exercise after cancer surgery.

"pursuit" of the believer. Every athlete pursues victory and keeps focused on that goal.

Chapter 12 of Hebrews is the practical application of the great truths this epistle presents about Jesus. Hebrews describes the wonderful truth about the uniqueness of Jesus, and chapter 12 uses the metaphor of running to show us the relevance of Jesus to our personal lives. The author of Hebrews must have watched endurance races—and known that the characteristics of an endurance athlete would be easily understood by those to whom he wrote.

We can find many parallels in the way God created us physically and the spiritual truths He gave through His Word. In addition to the author of Hebrews, the apostle Paul and the prophet Isaiah also communicate spiritual truth by pointing to the athlete.

When I first discovered this biblical perspective, I began speaking and writing about it. Many people were helped. But a few were skeptical.

One friend said, "The concept of distance running—all I see is a lot of pain, and no place to end the race (until we keel over and die)." He continued, "Part of it is the culture, the rat race, the keep-moving-at-all-cost mentality that has run me ragged. Part of it is that constant contradiction inherent in being a Christian. We are told to die to our own way. Die to our own selves. But most of us don't know what that means or what to replace it with. The thought of replacing it with an ongoing marathon race is not appealing to me. And not only that, it seems we are being asked to do something, sort of implying working (or running) for God's approval."

My friend has some reasonable objections. Most people are tired of being tired, and running seems like a lot of work—and pain. Discipline appears to fly in the face of grace.

Rather than ignore the imagery the Bible uses, we need to understand the truth it contains. God is good, and He loves us more than we will ever comprehend. All truth in His Word ultimately brings Him glory—and holds great benefits for us. The endurance metaphor isn't in the Bible to say you need more hardships. Instead, it shows us how to live by God's grace and power in the midst of adversities.

GRACE FOR THE RACE

Perhaps there's never been a person who understood and experienced God's grace like the apostle Paul. His writings are inspired by grace, laced with grace, and bestow grace on all who read them. Imagine you're with Dr. Luke as he visits Paul in a Roman dungeon not long before Paul is executed for his faith. As you enter the dark hole where Paul is kept, your stomach churns and you almost vomit from the stench. Only a few rays of light enable you to see the weary apostle. He looks decades older than he is.

When he sees Luke, he pulls him close and speaks softly. "Luke, our colleague Demas has forsaken us. The world's philosophy has captured his heart. He's departed from the simplicity and purity of devotion to Christ. It breaks my heart. I'm concerned about this generation of leaders."

Luke looks sympathetically into his eyes and tries to encourage him. "I know. But there are others who have stood firm, who have kept the faith. There are young men who love the Savior and also love you—like Timothy."

"Yes, Timothy," Paul says with a gentle smile. "I've written a letter to my young friend. You must make sure he reads it and understands what I'm saying. Luke, look at my face, my body. What do you see? They will soon kill me. I don't need anyone trying to make me feel good. Speak honestly."

With tears, Luke whispers, "Paul, I see an old soldier for Christ. I see the effects of suffering on your body. I see wisdom written in the wrinkles on your face and faithfulness in the scars on your back. I see a wounded warrior. I see a hero."

Paul replies with a firm but gentle voice. "Now, look into my eyes and tell me what you see. Look closely."

Just a few inches from Paul's face, Luke looks directly into his eyes. He can't believe what he sees. Though there's little light in the room, one ray shines directly into Paul's eyes. Luke stumbles in surprise. "I see light, beautiful light."

Paul smiles. "Yes, and that's what Timothy must know. Demas saw the pain, the suffering. It seemed unbearable to him, and he left us. Timothy has also seen my suffering, but he must know about the light."

After a pause, Paul begins again. "His dad loved the athletic games. Tell Timothy I've run the race. I've finished my course. It's been a difficult race, but one full of glory and grace. His grace has been sufficient. I've kept my eyes on the winner's crown, and now I'm about to receive it. Oh, the joy of the crown. Oh, the beauty of the crown. It's indescribable. Every beating—every difficulty is worth it because the crown awaits those who endure in this race. It's the light that pierces my eyes and into my soul. Tell Timothy to run and to finish well. Tell him about the light you see in my eyes."

➡ ➡ ➡ ➡ ➡ ➡

The race may have seemed difficult to Demas, but Paul knew that God's grace was displayed in the midst of difficulties. Likewise, many passages of Scriptures seem difficult to us—but once applied, they display the glory of God's grace. Jesus told His disciples to take His "yoke upon" them. That seemed difficult, but He told them, "My yoke is easy, and my burden is light" (Matthew 11:29, 30 ESV). Jesus also said, "Blessed are those who mourn, for they will be comforted" (Matthew 5:4). Both statements seem like contradictions. But once we apply those truths, the light of God's glory and grace supernaturally shine in our hearts. They produce a divine enablement that empowers us to climb the most difficult hills.

To my amazement, obedience to the word *run* not only produced incredible change in my life but also renewed my physical strength. Within three months of the doctor releasing me to run, I lost nearly 60 pounds and placed second in my age division in a half marathon in Baton Rouge. One year later, I completed the course of the original Greek Marathon. And one year after that, I won the gold medal in the 400 meters at the Texas State Senior Games.

Everything God promised in His Word came to pass as I sought to trust and obey Him. These Scriptures brought life and a deep conviction about the greatness of His grace.

I invite you to join me on a run through these fields filled with gemstones. Peek into the goldmine. The nuggets scattered along God's racecourse will enrich you, producing strength, endurance, and character. You will climb the most difficult hills—and end up stronger at the top. You'll learn how to run a well-thought-out, God-initiated pace in life. These nuggets will even teach you to develop a lifestyle that could improve your physical health.

God wants you to run like a champion. You may not feel like one. You may even think you face hardships that keep you from fulfilling your potential. These truths—and this story—are especially for you. You'll discover how to turn sorrow into joy and difficulty into triumph. But let me warn you: Get ready to run—and run a very long way.

pursuing the dream

… I was barely able to run and considered giving up. "Who am I to think I can actually go to the national championships and do well?" I thought. I didn't want to embarrass myself. Then Rick said something that changed me: "Have fun and let the clock be what it will." These words reminded me that the point was to pursue a lifelong dream and make it an adventure worth celebrating. Even as an adult, I'd been focusing on the end result instead of the journey. I decided then to make my dream a lifestyle, not a destination.[1]

Holly Hight in *Running Times* magazine

Pursue peace with everyone, and holiness, for without it no one will see the Lord.

Hebrews 12:14

"**N**o, seriously, why are you going to do this?" friends asked at my sixtieth birthday party. Everyone laughed because I had just told them the story of Pheidippides—and that I planned to run the same course. One month earlier I'd had cancer surgery, and I was still recuperating. A 60-year-old, overweight cancer survivor running the Athens Classic Marathon seemed unlikely. But my answer to that question was the most important part of preparing for the race.

Most great athletes have a clear answer to the "why" question. Often their purpose rises from a lifelong dream. Greatness demands discipline. Without the dream, discipline becomes too painful, and life too difficult. But with the *right kind of dream*, nothing is impossible. That's not the power of positive thinking but rather a proper understanding of biblical faith.

CHAMPIONS IN THE RACE

I love to read about champions because they're dreamers. Some of the greatest advice I ever received was through reading the biographies of great men and women of God. "Read their lives," a friend told me. "Study their habits. Dissect their character. Let them mentor you. Find out what made them great."

When Hebrews tells us to "run with endurance the race set out for us" (12:1), it first points to the great champions of the Bible and reminds us how they ran. The author wants us to know what produced their greatness.

After describing the wonder and beauty of Jesus in the first ten chapters, he then reminds us of people like Abel, Enoch, Noah, Sarah, Abraham, and Moses. All of them realized their dream by faith. Abel worshiped by faith. Enoch walked by faith. Noah worked by faith. Sarah birthed a child by faith. Abraham grew a family by faith. Moses delivered a nation by faith. By faith—and faith alone—these men and women ran like champions.

Something enables us to identify with their testimonies. Most of them experienced not only great difficulties but also glaring failures. After God saved his family, Noah consumed wine until he ended in a drunken stupor. Abraham was a great man of faith, but he laughed at the promise of God. Moses was the greatest prophet to arise in Israel but didn't make it into the Promised Land because his anger caused him to disobey God when he struck the rock. They were great men, but also men with great weaknesses.

Their greatness didn't lie in their ability to run the race. It wasn't their talent that made them great—it was their faith. The Bible doesn't put those men and women on a pedestal. They were people just like us—people who failed and had innate tendencies toward immorality and unbelief. But they overcame because they believed and trusted in Jesus. Just as we look back in time and trust in the Messiah, they looked forward in faith to the coming of the Messiah. The essence and uniqueness of Jesus is that God became Man in a point in time and human history. We trust in the historical Jesus just as the men and women of old trusted in a historical Jesus. He met their needs then and He meets our needs today.

Jesus said that Abraham saw His day and rejoiced in it (John 8:56). Every one of them believed that God would one day send a Messiah, and they trusted in Him.

The writer of Hebrews characterizes these men and women as those who have already run an endurance race—and who now watch us run. Their faith was focused and directed. It wasn't just an emotional or psychological state. It rose from a dream birthed from above and then descended into the depths of their hearts.

PERSONAL ENCOUNTERS

I've found it helps to meet someone, through literature or in person, who has seen God's dream and believed in Him to bring it to pass. Seeing their faith births greater faith. Not long ago, I became discouraged with running because I had been diagnosed with severe knee problems: a torn meniscus, a Baker's cyst, osteoarthritis, and inflammation. I didn't know if physically I could continue running. After three months of rest, I ventured back to the track to see if I could resume my exercise regimen.

While working out, I met a trainer working with a high school student. To my amazement, the trainer was Charles Austin, the American and Olympic record-holder for the high jump. I told him about my knee and the discouragement that came with it. He said, "I can help you." Before the 1996 Olympics in Atlanta, he'd had knee surgery. Doctors told Austin he would never be able to compete. But his dream refused to die. He watched the World Track and Field Championships on television and determined he wouldn't forsake his dream. To everyone's amazement, he won the gold medal and broke the Olympic record. His faith defied the odds.

When Austin told me his story, I wanted to know more about overcoming adversity. I, too, had a dream. Faith immediately rose in my heart. If Charles Austin could overcome an impossible situation and become the best high jumper in the world, then there was hope for me. (In a later chapter I will describe how Austin applied certain life principles to overcome those difficulties and jump higher than any other Olympian ever.)

When you meet someone who has run the race of life like a champion, you want to learn everything you can from that person. In 1970, I met such a person. Dr. Frank Laubach was nearly 90 years old and teaching at Asbury College. His life carried a sweet aroma of the presence of Christ. I don't think I had ever met anyone who reflected such Christlike character as Dr. Laubach. He was a great man of prayer and had been instrumental in developing a method of teaching literacy used by educators around the world.

I sat down with Dr. Laubach and said, "I'm a young minister. What can you tell me to help me serve the Lord?" He shared many truths, but one of the things he said was that he had prayed and dreamed for many years that he would see a great spiritual revival at Asbury College. Months before I met Dr. Laubach, God answered his prayer.

In February 1970, a normal chapel service at the school exploded into a spiritual revival. A service that normally lasted forty-five minutes went nonstop for seven days and nights. God's presence filled students. A sense of brokenness, repentance, and forgiveness permeated the campus. People flew to Lexington, Kentucky, from throughout the United States then drove to the Asbury campus to witness what was taking place. The spirit of revival swept across Christian universities and seminaries throughout America. Since then, I've met missionaries, pastors, professors, and Christian leaders all over the world who were touched by that great move of God.

Who would have dreamed that one forty-five minute chapel service would become the catalyst of a mighty revival on

Christian campuses throughout the United States? A champion would. Dr. Frank Laubach did.

THREE KINDS OF DREAMS

Not every dream contains the seeds for success. The source of the dream holds the key to victory. A dream has three possible sources. It can begin from *within, without,* or *above.* If you are to see your dream's fulfillment, it's critical to know where it originates.

Most people think the dream of a champion begins from within. I don't. I can dream about becoming the next Michael Jordan, but that will never happen. Why? God didn't place within me the same gifts and abilities as in Michael Jordan. No matter how much I visualize becoming a basketball superstar or how many hours I shoot hoops, I'll never be that kind of player.

We're often disappointed because we imagine becoming someone or doing something God never intended. Every person is uniquely and wonderfully made. We run our race to its fullest potential when we discover who we are—and become comfortable living in our own skin. The fulfillment of a dream doesn't begin with psyching yourself to do something you perceive is great. If the dream originates as merely something to satisfy your ego, you'll never become a true champion.

Dreams may also come from *without,* from others. We can dream someone else's dream—and never achieve God's potential for us. When my friend, Ken Leeburg, challenged me more than thirty years ago to run the course of the original

Greek Marathon, I was excited. We trained for a couple of years before he was tragically killed in an auto accident. When we went out for long runs, I always struggled to keep up with Ken. He had an endurance that came naturally. When I was about to quit on the hills, he was filled with energy, yelling, "Up the hill, over the hill, conquer the hill. Come on, Sam. You can make it." Halfway up the hill, I wanted to yell, "Give me a break."

But when we did speed work, that was a different story. My endurance and energy system kicked into overdrive. What felt difficult to Ken seemed easy to me. We would run 100-meter repeats, and Ken couldn't hang with me. That was my first hint that I was dreaming someone else's dream. When I ran the Greek Marathon, I ran for God's glory and to remember the life of my dear friend. But after I completed it, many people asked, "Are you going to run another one?" I replied, "I don't think so."

I knew it wasn't my race. If I was going to run to my full potential, I needed to discover the race God created me to run. I learned much by training for the Greek Marathon, and I've applied many of those truths. But I could achieve my running potential only by running the race He created me for. I could never run Ken's race and achieve my full potential. Many people spend their lives chasing someone else's dream. But much joy comes from discovering God's dream for you.

The third and greatest kind of dream is one that originates *above*, in God's heart. That dream produces the potential for you to run like a champion. There may be many things you do well but only one you do best. When you discover that one thing and pursue it, you will rise to heights you've never known.

Ryan Hall stands as one of the greatest long distance runners in U.S. history. On January 14, 2007, he became the first American to run a half marathon under one hour. He holds many titles: 2008 Olympic Trials Men's Marathon champion, 2007 U.S. Half Marathon champion, 2006 U.S.A. Cross Country champion, and 2005 NCAA 5,000 Meter champion.[2]

I discussed with Hall this thought of "dreaming God's dream." (The entire interview can be found in the Appendix.) Hall knew he had been gifted to run. When he was in college, he was determined to be "the best miler in the world." But he experienced one disappointment after another.

"It took a lot to finally bring me down to what God had for my running in terms of picking out an event," Hall said. "It came after a lot of heartbreak. I had a lot of bad races in college—came in last place race after race. I wasn't improving at all, and it was just a frustrating time. But that made me open up my hand to the gift that God gave me. I thought, 'All right, Lord, I don't care what event You want me to do. I just want to do what You've created me to do.' And when I came to that point, I was starting to experiment with the longer races and it came very natural to me. Afterwards, now looking back, I'm thinking, 'Man, I wish I would've gotten wise to that faster.'"

Ryan Hall became a champion when he opened himself to God's dream rather than his own. God's dreams hold much more potential because He created us, and He knows what is best for our lives.

GOD'S GIFTS CARRY GOD'S DREAM

When God calls you, He always *gifts* you. Both Ryan Hall and Charles Austin used the word *gift* when they described the pursuit of their dreams. They carry a deep sense that their abilities are gifts entrusted to them.

In the kingdom of God, we become champions when we run our race using the gifts He has given us. One way you can recognize that a dream comes from above is by realizing His provision always accompanies His call. One of my favorite verses in the Bible says, "He who calls you is trustworthy, and he will in fact do this" (1 Thessalonians 5:24).

The biblical image of the athlete reminds us that greatness in life is achieved by those who discern God's gifts and apply them by loving God and serving others. The question then arises, "How do you know which gifts you have been given?" The answer will bring you a long way in discerning God's plan. If we go to the image of running used in Hebrews and by the apostle Paul and Isaiah, we begin to comprehend His plan.

There are three basic types of runners: sprinters, middle distance, and long distance. The great sprinters have been created with more "fast twitch" muscle fibers, while long distance runners have more "slow twitch" muscle fibers. There is also a third type of muscle fiber that changes from "fast twitch" to "slow twitch" or vice versa, based on the runner's training. Every person is born with a different amount of muscle fiber types. That's why Charles Austin and Ryan Hall were very accurate in describing their abilities as gifts. They had nothing to do with the types of muscle fibers with which they were born. That was a gift from God. Yes, those athletes needed to develop those gifts to achieve greatness. But without the gift, they could never have accomplished what they did. Only when Hall decided to switch to long distance rather than middle distance did he taste greatness.

DISCERNING GOD'S PLAN

So how does a person recognize when a dream descends from heaven? How do you discern whether it is your idea, someone else's, or God's dream for your life?

Devastating failure became the doorway to incredible success for Ryan Hall because it opened him to God's leadership. This openness is the first step to understanding God's plan and gifting for your life. The apostle Paul wrote to believers in Rome about the gifts of God's Spirit. But he first said, "Therefore I exhort you, brothers and sisters, by the mercies of God, to present your bodies as a sacrifice—alive, holy, and pleasing to God—which is your reasonable service" (Romans 12:1). When we surrender ourselves to God, we're saying we trust Him with our lives. It's an act of faith—admitting we believe He's good and knows what's best for us.

Faith places us in a position to know the will of God, but then we must pursue His plan for our lives. When Ryan Hall opened his hand to the gift God gave him, he also experimented with different distances. Hall didn't recognize the gift while sitting in a dorm room doing nothing. He knew he had a gift for running, and he wanted to know specifically how to apply that gift.

Many people wait for some mystical revelation of their gifting. But I've discovered it's much easier to change directions in a moving vehicle than in one sitting idle. The purpose of God's gifting is for His glory and the benefit of others. So we're most likely to recognize His gifting when we are doing something that brings Him glory and also helps other people. When you get out and begin doing something, the discovery process begins.

As you begin pursuing God's dream for your life, a deep sense of joy will rise in your heart as you use your gifts. But beware of the deceptive and discouraging practice of comparing ourselves to others. We often miss God's best because we hold one of two attitudes: we're the best, or we're the worst. We become deceived when we think, "I'm better than others." And we become discouraged when we think, "I'm not good enough."

After I ran the Greek Marathon, I wanted to begin experimenting to discover the race I was gifted to run. That's when I became involved in the Senior Games and U.S.A. Masters Track and Field. I didn't know where to start. So I tried everything. There was a local track meet in San Antonio where I live. I signed up for the 100 meters, 400 meters, 800 meters, and 1500 meters. It sounded crazy, but I wanted to find out which one of those races was mine. I finished second to last in the 100 and 400 but finished third in the 800 and 1500. Based on that, I decided to train for the 800 and 1500. It sounded good in theory but proved to be wrong.

A few months later, I planned to run both those distances in the Texas Masters Track and Field Championships. But after running the 800 meters, my lungs burned so badly I couldn't run another race. They didn't burn for just a few minutes. They burned for several days. That seemed strange. As I trained for the 800 and 1500 meters, I found myself dreading the workouts. But when I did shorter speed workouts, they felt natural. After the Masters meet, I decided to try to run shorter: the 400 and 800. A couple of months later, I ran in Utah at the Huntsman World Senior Games. The same burning sensation happened when I ran the 800 meters. Fortunately, the 400 meters was held on a different day. When I ran it, I won the bronze medal, though I had spent only a few weeks training for it. I realized that must be my race.

After the race in Utah, I visited a sports medicine doctor who diagnosed me with "exercise-induced asthma." The asthma kicked in around 600 meters. I wasn't created to run the 800. My mistake came because in the San Antonio meet I had done well in comparison to others in the longer distances. I eventually realized that was because I had built a high level of endurance by having run the Greek Marathon; it had nothing to do with the way God created me.

After Utah, I had only four weeks to train for the 400 meters in the Texas State Senior Games. Once I began working from my gifting, everything changed. I felt a sense of joy in running that I had never known. Faith rose in my heart, and discouragement fled. I won the gold medal at the state championship, finishing ahead of the guys who finished far ahead of me in San Antonio. But it didn't matter whether I won the Texas Senior Games or lost. I had found the race that would enable me to run to my greatest potential. I learned a

Sammy wins the 400 meters at the Texas Senior Games

great lesson. If you run a particular race because you're better than others, you will either become conceited or exhausted. But when you run the race to which God has called you, you run like a champion—no matter how you compare to others.

When you run according to your gifting, you may encounter problems along the way, but you feel a sense of joy and peace in the midst of the race. You experience a sense of fulfillment. It seems supernaturally natural.

GOD'S GIFTING AND GOD'S CHARACTER

There's one final, critical element we must understand if we are to run the race to our maximum potential. The race is not about pursuing the gift. The gift is God's divine enabling in the pursuit, but it is not what we pursue. The gift is a vehicle that transports us to the finish line. It plays a definite role in pursuing the dream, but it is not the dream. That's why the question

I was asked at my birthday party was so critical: "Why are you doing this?"

The Bible clearly states what the pursuit of the race is in Hebrews 12:14: "Pursue peace with everyone, and holiness, for without it no one will see the Lord." Thus, our pursuit in the Christian life is twofold. We pursue a right relationship with all people and a growing relationship with God, which is holiness. If you want to see God in His manifest glory, you must pursue this purpose.

After the apostle Paul wrote to the Roman believers about the gifts of the Spirit, he warned them about two things: "Do not be conceited" (Romans 12:16), and "If possible, so far as it depends on you, live peaceably with all people" (Romans 12:18). It takes humility to pursue peace with others, especially when you feel you've been wronged. But humility places us on the path to holiness.

If our pursuit is holiness, we need to understand its nature. *Holy* means "set apart." Only one person is completely holy: Jesus. He stands in a category all His own. That's what the author of Hebrews was communicating throughout the entire book. But he closes by challenging the reader to "pursue holiness." In other words, the pursuit of our lives must be Christlikeness.

That process begins the moment we receive Christ into our lives by faith and continues until the day we die. That's why champions are not made overnight. That's what was so attractive about Dr. Laubach. Though he died a few months after I met him, the fragrance of his life continues to this day. He was a man who gave his life and used all his gifts in the pursuit of becoming like Christ. That kind of person finishes a winner.

Likewise, when I interviewed Ryan Hall, what I found most impressive was not his accomplishments but his pursuit. "I felt like God told me that He had given me a gift, and that gift is to be used to help other people," he said. "So I run to accomplish that. And, in pursuing that, I find fullness of life and fullness of joy—which is what I think we're all looking for. I feel like I've accomplished the mission that God has given me, and I'll continue to go down this running path that I have been on for the last thirteen years."

Hall isn't just in pursuit of gold medals. He's in pursuit of the truth laced with gold. You may not be a Frank Laubach or a Ryan Hall, but you are uniquely and wonderfully created. You have a race to run. When you dream His dream and exercise your unique gifts in pursuit of His purpose, you will grow more into the image of Christ. You'll run like a champion.

---

1. Holly Hight, "Better Than the Dream," *Running Times,* March 2009, 44.

2. http://www.usatf.org/athletes/bios/hall_ryan.asp (accessed November 29, 2010)

shedding pounds

Endurance athletes … know that excess body fat is the enemy of performance in every endurance sport.[1]
Matt Fitzgerald in *Racing Weight*

Therefore, since we are surrounded by such a great cloud of witnesses, we must get rid of every weight and the sin that clings so closely, and run with endurance the race set out for us.
Hebrews 12:1

A few months before I ran the Greek Marathon, I took my grandchildren to a local park where I often work out. A jogger came by as I held the two younger ones. Together the kids weighed about 60 pounds—about the amount I lost in preparing for the marathon. When I saw the jogger I thought, *It would be impossible to run a marathon carrying these two kids. I couldn't run 26 yards, much less 26 miles.* Yet if I had tried to run the Greek Marathon without losing 60 pounds, that's exactly what I would have attempted. Shedding excess weight is a simple but basic principle for any athlete, especially the endurance athlete.

Weight loss. Those words cause most of us to roll our eyes thinking, *Not again. I know I need this, but it never lasts.* When I met with the cancer surgeon, he didn't tell me to run. He told me to lose weight and build endurance. It was God who placed the word *run* in my heart. That produced the chicken or egg question. Which came first—losing weight or running? The answer was simple: both.

As I searched the Scriptures about the athlete, two separate but closely connected concerns emerged. Both related to weight loss and had spiritual ramifications. One was the athletic metaphor; the other was a spiritual issue that needed to be addressed on a physical level. Matt Fitzgerald, an expert in endurance sports nutrition, writes, "Because there is so much overlap between running fitness and general health, virtually every factor that has a positive effect on your health is likely to have a positive effect on your running fitness."[2] The athletic metaphor about running with endurance will often overlap principles about our health.

THE BIBLE AND WEIGHT MANAGEMENT

Athletic metaphor

When the author of Hebrews wrote metaphorically about an endurance race, the first truth he highlighted was excess weight. The biblical image of the endurance race in Hebrews 12:1 illustrates practical Christian living and uses athletic imagery: "Get rid of *every weight and the sin* that clings so closely, and run with endurance the race set out for us" (emphasis added).

Spiritual truth with physical application

The weight loss imagery also reminds us of biblical truths that should cause us to evaluate how we treat our bodies. Paul twice asked the Christians in Corinth, "Do you not know that you are God's temple?" He then said, "God's temple is holy, which is what you are," and summed up his thoughts with, "Therefore glorify God with your body" (1 Cor. 3:16–17; 6:20). We live in a time and a cultural context that requires us to seriously consider weight management in light of these passages.

Before my cancer diagnosis, most people would not have described me as obese. They would have said I was overweight, even though clinical tests confirmed my obesity. I often rationalized my situation by thinking, "I'm this way because I'm serving God." My packed schedule, poor eating habits, and lack of exercise were a part of a flawed view of what it meant to glorify God.

THE NECESSITY OF REPENTANCE

I desperately needed a change of thinking, habits, and direction. There's a biblical term to describe that kind of change: *repentance*. But it's often viewed from a negative perspective. Repentance is not a word God uses to knock us over the head to let us know we've messed up. To the contrary, it's a term that sets us on the path of fulfilling His ultimate purpose.

When Peter preached in the book of Acts, he called for repentance, promising that the people would experience two things: forgiveness and times of refreshing from the presence of the Lord (Acts 3:19–20). Both are characteristics of spiritual renewal. Repentance is that change of heart, direction, and thinking that releases God's Spirit to apply His grace to our wounded hearts and to spark spiritual renewal in our lives. It returns us to our pursuit of Christlikeness.

When the author of Hebrews challenged believers to run their race, he said they must let go of *sin* and *every weight* that keeps them from developing endurance. Both issues are critical if we're to pursue conformity to the image of Christ. We can't hang on to certain attitudes, actions, and habits if we're going to run with endurance the race of becoming like Christ.

Three key words summarize repentance: *change, heart,* and *lifestyle.*

Change

If our pursuit as a follower of Jesus is becoming like Him, then change must be a constant part of our lives. We receive His nature when we receive Him into our lives. We must then continually be open to the lifelong transforming work of Christ.

Many people know they need to change their habits but don't seem to have the power or the knowledge to do so. Others seem satisfied with their level of growth. Either way, many settle into a lifestyle that ultimately robs them of a higher quality of life—and even limits their service for Christ. If we are to become like Christ, we must have a deep commitment to being changed by God's power.

Heart

During my last annual physical exam, my physician asked me, "What produced the change?" For more than two decades, he had encouraged me to lose weight. But that kind of change was never a priority. Like an accordion, my body expanded and deflated depending on the diet I attempted. After my cancer diagnosis and treatment, I not only lost nearly 60 pounds, but I finally kept it off.

My answer was simple. At the moment of the cancer diagnosis, it became a heart issue, not just another resolution at the beginning of the year. I became honest on a much deeper level and had to ask, "How was I treating my body (God's temple), and what were the ramifications?"

Paul's exhortation to the Christians in Rome reminded me to present my body as a living sacrifice to God (Romans 12:1). The verse concludes by saying, "which is your reasonable service." That part of the Scripture produced genuine repentance (change). I had not glorified God with my body. The passion of my life has been to bring glory to Him, and I knew I had failed. That deep conviction produced a turning in my heart—from an unhealthy to a healthy lifestyle. I learned to worship God by surrendering my body to Him. Starting that day I no longer treated my body the way I had previously. It became a heart issue even more than a health issue.

Successful Christian living always begins with the heart. When I interviewed Ryan Hall, he described how important attitudes were to his success. "I've spent so much time training my physical body," he said, "but I'm constantly telling myself the most important thing I can train is my heart. And I really believe it's the heart that drives the body. And it's the heart that enables us to endure whatever's thrown at us…. It's really the determining factor in life."

Lifestyle

Like many Americans, I've tried several weight loss plans and was very successful. But there's a huge difference between losing weight and maintaining the loss. I could never keep it off. Over the years, I must have cumulatively lost hundreds of pounds, but the fat always came roaring back.

What was the difference this time? I can describe it in one word: *lifestyle*. Repentance must be rooted in a desire to change our lifestyles, not just lose weight. Our hearts must cry out, "I want to develop a lifestyle that honors Christ by living in a healthy manner."

But how does a person develop a healthy lifestyle? Because no two people are alike, there's no single solution. Some people have genetic challenges that others don't. One person may gain weight rapidly because of a genetic disposition, while another burns fat quickly. There's also the issue of God's sovereignty. He gives and takes away. Some people live longer than others, and there's nothing anyone can do to change that. I've lost three close friends in accidents. All three attempted to glorify God with their bodies. Yet they all died young. There are things in life we can't control. Still, it's imperative that we make sure we're not shortening our lives by abusing our bodies.

Christians rightfully point to addictions such as alcohol and drugs as abuse. But many of us seem blind to a more subtle abuse of our bodies—becoming overweight. The average weight of a person has become a major health issue in America. The U.S. Centers for Disease Control (CDC) in a 2009 report on obesity stated, "More than one third of U.S. adults—more than 72 million people—and 16% of U.S. children are obese. Since 1980, obesity rates for adults have doubled and rates for children have tripled."[3]

Dr. Gil Kaats, director of the Health and Medical Research Center in San Antonio, Texas, attended the American Medical Association's "Summit on Obesity" in 2004 and reported that "dysfunctional body composition" is a "powerful accelerator of over

40 different diseases." [4] The CDC in its 2009 report listed some health consequences of obesity, including "coronary heart disease; type 2 diabetes; cancers (endometrial, breast, and colon); hypertension (high blood pressure); dyslipidemia (for example, high total cholesterol or high levels of triglycerides); stroke; liver and gallbladder disease; sleep apnea and respiratory problems; osteoarthritis (a degeneration of cartilage and its underlying bone within a joint); gynecological problems (abnormal menses, infertility)." [5]

When I asked Dr. Kaats about weight loss, he said, "You're going to have to make the changes in your lifestyle that are compatible with what you're going to do the rest of your life. In short, do not lose weight with anything you're not willing to do for the rest of your life." If we are going to take a serious look at the race to which God has called us, we must take a serious look at developing a healthy lifestyle.

When the author of Hebrews wrote about getting "rid of every weight and the sin that clings so closely," there was probably no thought given to a worldwide obesity plague in the twenty-first century. But the context of the passage deals with much more than health. It uses the athletic metaphor to challenge us to live the Christian life to our full potential. It calls us to remove two specific but separate things that weigh us down and keep us from running with endurance: *sin* and *every weight.*

GETTING RID OF SIN

If becoming like Jesus is the goal of our race, then it's an absolute necessity to remove anything in our lives that displeases God. There's no wiggle room with this truth. The uniqueness of Jesus, presented throughout the book of Hebrews, is rooted in His purity. He had everything in common with us—except that He was without sin. He dotted every i and crossed every t in His obedience to the Father.

We can't cling to sin and still become like Christ. We must have a deep commitment to follow His plan—and when we fail, we must be quick to confess our failure and repent (change). We can't wallow in the misery that comes from failure and expect to become like Christ.

Repentance calls for honesty, confession, and letting go. *Honesty* requires humility, which releases God's grace to heal and restore the wounds wrought by our failures. *Confession* is much more than saying, "I'm sorry." Rather, it's saying, "I'm wrong." To grow in Christ, we must be willing to admit, "I've been wrong." Confession is built upon humility. It carries with it a willingness to admit to God, others, and ourselves that we have been wrong in our attitudes, actions, or lack of actions.

The third element of repentance is *letting go.* Some people confess to God with all intentions of returning to the wrong attitude or action. But if we're to become like Christ, we must let go. We can't hold on to those things that clearly displease God and still run with endurance. I could never run the Greek Marathon with 60 excess pounds, and you'll never run to your full potential by carrying sinful habits and attitudes.

EVERY WEIGHT THAT CLINGS SO CLOSELY

Some habits aren't necessarily sin, but they keep us from running to our full potential. It might not be sin to watch television or a sporting event. But if a person becomes so absorbed in them that they neglect their intimacy with God or time with their families, they've developed a lifestyle that keeps them from becoming like Christ. These are often the most difficult things to recognize and remove because they're not black-and-white issues.

It's also possible that others see us as "godly" people because we have dealt with many of the "sin" issues. Yet we carry excess weight that keeps us from becoming all that God intends. We become satisfied with having achieved a certain level of spiritual maturity. We may not commit some horrible sin, but other things hinder us from growing in Christ. Others may pat us on the back and tell us how inspiring we are. Yet deep within we know we've ceased growing in our walk with God. To others we look spiritually fit, but we run far below our God-given potential because we've become self-satisfied.

After I completed the Greek Marathon and decided to run the 400 meters in the U.S.A. Masters Track and Field, people kept telling me how impressed they were with my weight loss. "Sammy, you don't need to lose any more weight," some said. "You look great the way you are."

Then I started working out with a couple of other Masters Track and Field guys. Our trainer would occasionally film us. As we watched the video to evaluate our form, something jumped out: I was heavier than the other guys. I wondered if I needed to lose more weight. But I kept hearing, "You look great, Sammy. Don't lose any more weight." I believed that until one night while working out at my home.

Normally when I work out I wear a shirt. But because I was in my home, I was wearing only running shorts. I took a prone plank position (my body straight with my toes and my elbows touching the ground). While holding that position, I looked down and saw something that sent shock waves through me. Two big clumps of fat were hanging from my belly! I screamed, and my wife came running into the room. Tex looked at me (still in my prone plank position) and said, "What's wrong?"

"Honey, get down on the floor and look at my stomach and tell me what you see."

Like the sweet wife that she is, Tex knelt, looked, ... and began roaring with laughter.

I got up and said, "Okay, you get in the prone position."

Still laughing, she complied with my request.

I pulled up her blouse and looked: No fat was hanging from her belly. I rolled over moaning, while she stood laughing.

"I need to lose more weight," I said, groaning.

She kissed me on the cheek and walked away—smiling.

That was my first indicator I was still carrying excess weight. A few months later, science confirmed my observation. I read a book by Dr. Massimo Testa, a renowned sports doctor who worked with Olympian Eric Heiden. After Heiden won five gold medals in the 1980 Winter Olympics, he became a champion cyclist and received a medical degree from Stanford University. Dr. Testa met Heiden after a race in Europe and in 1985 became the team physician for America's 7-Eleven professional cycling team. Dr. Testa devised a different approach to training and convinced some of the Americans to follow his training regimen. In his book with Eric Heiden, *Faster, Better, Stronger*, Dr. Testa describes what took place:

Team 7-Eleven went on to astonish the European cycling world with stage wins in the Giro d'Italia and Tour de France. It gradually shifted the axis of American professional cycling, and thus reflected on America's showings in the international arena today. A young and talented Lance Armstrong joined the team and won the world championship in 1993, and the rest is history.[6]

As I read Dr. Testa and Eric Heiden's book, a crazy idea popped into my head. I tried to contact Dr. Testa about my training. Incredibly, I found a telephone number. Dr. Testa's assistant was out working with the U.S. Olympic team when I called, so Dr. Testa answered the phone. I told him who I was and that I was beginning to train for U.S. Masters Track and Field. He invited me to visit his office and said he would do some testing to evaluate my fitness level and give me some advice to improve my training. I was elated.

When I met Dr. Testa, he told me he needed to give me a thorough physical exam before he could test my oxygen and lactic acid levels. After going through the normal medical procedures, he said, "I need to do a body fat ratio test." He took his calipers and pinched my shoulders, biceps, quads, calves, and chest. I felt pretty good until he aimed the calipers at my stomach. I knew what was waiting there—my two clumps of fat! As my eyes followed the calipers, the instrument opened wider and wider until it was able to grab one of those big bulges. My smile fell.

Dr. Testa recorded all of the numbers and did some calculations. He showed me a chart, saying, "Mr. Tippit, this chart shows several levels of body fat composition. The first level is obesity. The next, overweight. Then, healthy. Fourth, very fit. Then, athlete. And finally, elite athlete. Your test results show you are healthy, even very fit. But if you want to run as an athlete—that is, run to your full potential—you're going to have to get rid of some excess body fat." I heeded his words, and they put me on the road to winning the gold medal at the Texas State Senior Games.

Many believers need to go into the Great Physician's exam room and allow Him to measure the excess weight we carry. Our friends may tell us, "You're a great Christian. Just keep doing what you've been doing. You don't need to change." But the Great Physician will speak the truth in love to our hearts.

He may say, "If you want to live at your full potential, you must get rid of some things that aren't necessarily sin but keep you from becoming like Christ."

The person who follows His instructions will live like a champion and discover a new measure of gold—becoming more like Jesus.

---

1. Matt Fitzgerald, *Racing Weight* (Boulder, Colorado: Velo Press, 2009), 3.
2. Matt Fitzgerald, *Performance Nutrition for Runners* (Emmaus, Pennsylvania: Rodale Publishers, 2006), 4.
3. http://www.cdc.gov/chronicdisease/resources/publications/aag/obesity.htm (accessed November 29, 2010).
4. http://www.cdc.gov/obesity/causes/health.html (accessed November 29, 2010).
5. http://www.cdc.gov/obesity/causes/health.html (accessed November 29, 2010).
6. Eric Heiden and Massimo Testa, *Faster, Better, Stronger: 10 Proven Secrets to a Healthier Body in 12 Weeks* (New York: William Morrow, 2008), xvi.

waiting to run

Ryan Hall believes he was chosen by
God to run for God. One of Hall's favorite Bible verses—the one he scribbled
on the autographed poster just inside the
door of the Teddy Bear Restaurant in Big Bear
Lake—is from the book of Isaiah. Those who wait
on the Lord, will run and not get tired. The Lord has
taught Hall not to overlook that key word: wait.[1]
Michael Perry in *Runners World* magazine

… Those who wait for the Lord's help find renewed strength;
they rise up as if they had eagles' wings, they run without growing weary, they walk without getting tired.
Isaiah 40:31

Though there has been much scientific research in recent years
about running, the basic principles remain constant. Athletes
continue to practice those training truths. But one truth seems
particular to the Christian athlete. It was highlighted in the
movie *Chariots of Fire* and discussed in a *Runners World* article
about Ryan Hall.

Both Hall and Eric Liddell were champions who discovered
the biblical truth in Isaiah 40:31: waiting on the Lord. It played a
vital role in their success. The Scripture promises that God will
renew our strength when we wait on Him. It declares that we
will not only "rise up as if [we] had eagles' wings" but also *"run*

without growing weary." Many Christians understand this truth to have spiritual rather than physical significance. While Hall and Liddell grasped the truth metaphorically, they also applied it literally.

In my interview with Hall, I asked him about the Boston Marathon. He had written in a blog that he felt joy in the midst of the pain during Boston. I said the two concepts seemed contradictory.

"When you're in His presence, there's so much joy," Hall said. "What I pray when I'm out there racing and going through those hard times is just to be in the presence of God. I want to find a way to connect with Him in those hard moments because whenever I'm in His presence I always feel the joy. I think that's the best way to find joy—just to connect and to be in His presence."

Finding strength and joy in God's presence. That simple truth was also embraced by Eric Liddell, the 400-meter world champion in 1924. *Chariots of Fire* was not a movie produced for a Christian audience but for the general population. But when the producers researched Liddell's life, they discovered a truth that lay at the heart of the champion: waiting to run. A scene immediately before the Olympics depicts Liddell quoting the Isaiah passage. That same truth propelled both Liddell and Hall to run like champions, though they lived and ran in different centuries.

Most people read that verse in Isaiah with thoughts of spiritual renewal. It's certainly that. But Hall's and Liddell's experiences should cause us to ask an important question: Does waiting on the Lord enable people to achieve their maximum potential—and possibly even beyond their potential? It would be an interesting question for scientific research. Logically, it doesn't seem too far of a stretch to conclude that "waiting on the Lord" can produce extraordinary results. If the God who created us lives inside us, and our bodies are the dwelling place of His Spirit, then it makes sense that we would live at our maximum potential when we are filled with His presence.

WAIT FOR THE PROMISE

Perhaps the greatest illustration of both renewal and running at maximum potential can be found throughout the Acts of the Apostles. The last thing Jesus told His disciples to do was to "wait [in Jerusalem] for what my Father promised" (Acts 1:4).

The first thing we discover in Acts is that the believers are waiting in a spirit of prayer in an upper room in Jerusalem, just as Jesus commanded. The Holy Spirit descends upon that small band of men and women—and 3,000 people are converted. In the next chapter, Peter and John are going to a prayer meeting—and a lame man is healed. In chapter four, the church is once again in a prayer meeting, waiting on the Lord. The Holy Spirit fills them, and they speak with power and boldness.

We find this pattern throughout Acts. The church prays. Then it proclaims. That was the strategy of Jesus: Wait for God's presence and then proclaim His name. As long as believers followed that example, cities, nations, and the Roman Empire were impacted.

Realize who these early Christians were. They weren't the noblemen or educators of their day. They weren't the rich and famous. They weren't great orators. They were simple, humble, ordinary men and women. Who were they? Cowards and doubters before the coming of the Holy Spirit—but champions after His presence filled their lives.

Imagine you are in that upper room after the ascension of Jesus. Your companions are a group of men and women who walked with Jesus for three years, including Peter, who denied Jesus; Thomas, who doubted Him; and Matthew, a tax collector.

Peter, who never seems able to hide his emotions, paces the room. Worry is written on his face. He lifts his hands in exasperation, telling Thomas, "I'm afraid, confused, and unsure of everything. I know that He is truly the Messiah. But I failed Him so badly. I denied Him, not once but three times. How can I tell others who He is and what He can do for them?"

Thomas grabs Peter. "You denied Him, and I doubted Him. But He forgave us. I don't understand how our lives could be instruments that would bring glory to Him. It seems impossible. But I believe with my whole heart that His words are true. He said to wait and the promise of His Father would come upon us." Thomas shakes Peter. Looking eyeball to eyeball, he says, "Peter, we must wait. He will let us know what to do. We must simply obey Him. He will give us the power. If He doesn't saturate us with His presence, what can we do? We have no power within ourselves to do anything. Our only hope is that He fills us with His power from on high."

Peter and Thomas walk to a corner and kneel. They wait—not knowing what to think or expect. They remain frozen in silence.

Soon afterward, the day of Pentecost arrives—and a mighty rushing wind fills the room. God's fire falls on that small band of uneducated men and women. The presence of His Spirit engulfs everyone. Such ecstasy. Such joy inside that room. Confusion erupts outside as devout Jews from around the world hear these commoners praying—but each hears in his own national language. The natural becomes supernatural.

Peter, the common fisherman and trembling coward, stands in the middle of the crowd and speaks. Never before an orator, he now eloquently proclaims the death, burial, and resurrection of Jesus. He speaks with power and authority. A spiritual explosion erupts. The ordinary turns into the extraordinary. Thousands place their faith in the Messiah. A movement is birthed that will shape human history. Every nation, tribe, and race will forever be affected by what happened that day.

The story doesn't conclude with one moment of greatness but continues throughout the book of Acts. The strategy of this small group was simple: wait and run, pray and proclaim. People of the day said they "turned the world upside down" (Acts 17:6 ESV). Look throughout the history of the church and you'll discover the same pattern when great revival movements spread. Renewal within—and extraordinary works without—accompany those who wait to run.

FORCED TO WAIT

From the days of the early church until today, nations have been transformed by those who learned to wait on the Lord. Yet waiting to run isn't just for those who spark great national revivals. It's the way each of us pursues our ultimate purpose in life. It's how we run our individual races. If God can take a coward like Peter, what will He do with you when you wait for Him? He will turn the hearts of fathers to their sons and the sons to their fathers. He will heal broken marriages and turn bitterness into forgiveness. He will renew our strength and revive our souls. We will run like champions.

I discovered both the metaphoric and the literal application of this truth after my cancer surgery. I experienced a level of waiting on God that I had never known, and it produced the greatest revival of my life.

Telling me I would have a lot of down time while recovering from surgery, people sent me books and DVDs. But I knew God had a plan because prostate cancer was in my genes. One grandfather died of prostate cancer, and the other was diagnosed with it but died during surgery. I felt that God allowed me to discover my cancer before it was too late. I knew I needed to make this a time of waiting on the Lord, reading my Bible, and talking to God.

Instead of books and videos, I needed *The Book* and *His Presence*. I sought Him, and it was incredible. The presence of God filled my soul as I have never known. I didn't travel for three months but spent those days in solace. There were times I basked in the presence of God. Those minutes turned into hours, the hours became days, and the days became weeks. For three months, God's presence flooded my soul as I waited for Him.

Those times of refreshing began after I had a dream one night—the first night after I returned from the hospital. I don't build my life on dreams but on the truths in God's Word. But I believe that God can use dreams. He certainly used this one. In that dream, I saw two Native Americans: a small boy and an old man. They were sitting on a hill and staring across some field into the distance. Then two words began to echo: "Wounded Deer. Wounded Deer." The words kept resounding—louder and louder.

When I awoke the next morning, those words kept ringing in my head. I couldn't shake them. I asked God, "What is this 'wounded deer' dream about?" Then the scripture came to my heart from Psalm 42:1, "As a deer longs for streams of water, so I long for you, O God!" Then it hit me. I was like a wounded deer. My only hope was to go to the waters and drink from them deeply. Healing, refreshing, and strength were in the waters.

Scripture often uses "rivers of waters" to describe the presence of the Holy Spirit in our lives. I knew that God was telling me to wait at the place of the waters, to drink deeply from His presence.

I gave myself to drinking daily from those waters. During that time, the presence of God overwhelmed me. When I lay in bed, I read the Scriptures. Every verse seemed to leap off the page into my heart. God's Word became food for my hungry heart. A fresh loaf was delivered every hour. My kids gave me an iPod for Christmas, and I transferred all my worship music to it. I slowly limped from the living room to the bedroom—back and forth—worshiping Jesus Christ. I cried. I shouted. I laughed. I stood still in awe of His majesty. I sensed a renewed direction for my life.

A NEW DIRECTION

During that time I began to pray and think seriously about Ken's challenge to run the course of the ancient Greek Marathon. If God renewed my strength, I could "run without growing weary." I knew that to run the Greek Marathon, I first needed to prove to myself that I could run a half marathon. It seemed ridiculous.

I searched the Internet for a half marathon I could run— and found one. The minute I read about it, I knew I wanted to run it: the Baton Rouge Beach Half Marathon. The course ran through the LSU campus and around the nearby lakes. Somehow I knew I needed to run that half marathon as my trial race for the Greek Marathon. There was only one problem, but it was a major one. The Baton Rouge Beach Half Marathon was sched- uled for December 1, 2007—only three and a half months from the time the doctor released me to begin an exercise routine.

During the surgery, they cut my stomach muscles. The sur- geon said I should not begin any kind of exercise routine for the first six weeks. That took me to the middle of August. I also had *plantar fasciitis,* an inflammation in one foot that made even walking painful. I didn't know how long it would take to get over that. The surgery had taken place the end of June. After I came out of the surgery, they told me they had found cancer in the margins. This meant they didn't know if they removed all the cancer—or if some still remained in my body.

The surgery also produced another problem. For a long time my right arm was suspended upward so tubes could feed me intravenously. That produced stress on my shoulder and caused much pain and some complications. So I also needed therapy for my shoulder. The best description of my physical condition was that of a wounded deer.

Running the Baton Rouge Beach Half Marathon seemed impossible. I knew I would need at least three months' training before I could even attempt it. That meant I needed to begin training by the first of September. Because of my injuries, it seemed implausible.

As I spent time in prayer, God continued to speak to my heart. "Wait to run" echoed through my soul. That's how I run the race. Wait. Then run. Spend time with God. Drink from the waters and then run. I knew that was a literal interpretation of Isaiah 40:31 and Psalm 42:1, which spoke about renewing the heart. God had certainly renewed my heart, but was it possible He would also renew my body? Was it possible that if I waited for Him, I would literally "run without growing weary?"

The more I read the Scriptures, the more I realized that this was God's way. He often places us in impossible situations so we are forced to depend on Him. That causes us to wait for His strength. Those situations build faith and character. They produce champions.

WAITING, THEN TRAINING

I decided to attempt this great experiment. I would wait for the Lord before I attempted my physical conditioning. The physical conditioning, however, didn't begin with running but with more medical treatment. Before the doctor released me to exercise, I began seeing a sports therapist for the *plantar fasciitis*. I slept with a boot on my foot every night for several weeks. The boot stretched the bottom of my foot as I slept. I did stretching exercises every day and purchased orthotic inserts for my running shoes. I did everything possible to bring healing to my foot. The rest was in God's hands. I still needed healing of my stomach muscles and therapy for my shoulder. The shoulder therapy would have to wait until after the half marathon. And I prayed for no internal complications from the surgery.

The picture was pretty gloomy. If God did not renew me after my cancer surgery, it would be impossible to run the half marathon. I went to a local track in San Antonio to see if I could run any distance. I was encouraged. I walked and jogged very slowly one and a half miles. I walked most of the way, but at least I could do that.

I began training the first full week of September 2007 for the Baton Rouge Beach Half Marathon. I spent time in prayer and waiting on God. I then jogged very slowly, walked, and jogged very slowly again. I repeated this throughout the entire workout. Over the next few weeks I gradually built my mileage. By the end of six weeks, I could jog/walk/jog for six miles on my long run each Saturday.

I felt stronger as each day passed. God continued to renew my strength. I told Tex, "I think I'm going to be able to make it. And I believe it will be faster than I first thought." The more I waited and ran, the more confident I became. Faith was taking root in my heart. I ultimately built my mileage for my weekly long run to 10 miles.

TOWARD THE FINISH LINE

The test finally came. Tex and I flew to Baton Rouge. I was nervous that Saturday morning. But the weather looked great. It was in the upper 50s and the sun was shining. The sun's reflection off the LSU lakes was inspirational, the conditions perfect. I felt strong and believed I would be able to finish—but knew I still had potential for disaster with my foot, stomach, and shoulder. Tex and I found a private place to pray and commit the race to the Lord.

Hundreds of people lined up to start. My stomach was churning when the gun sounded. My adrenaline started pumping as I ran. I made the mistake most novices make: I started too fast. I knew after the first mile that I wouldn't be able to maintain that pace. I settled down and slowed my pace. But it was still faster than I had planned. At the five mile point, I saw Tex filming me. I wouldn't see her again until I finished.

I couldn't believe my pace for the first eight miles. I was running much faster than I anticipated, and I still felt strong. But after 10 miles I began to tire. That was the longest I had run during my training. The good news was that I felt confident I would finish. That was critically important. If I completed a half marathon, I could train to run the course of the ancient Greek Marathon and see the dream fulfilled.

The last three miles were not fun. But the closer I came to the end of the race, the lighter my heart grew. Then I saw it: the finish line. "Thank you, Lord," I whispered. Tex was cheering as I came across the line. I finished full of emotion but too exhausted to express it.

I hugged Tex and said, "I did it. I finished. By the grace of God, I finished." We grabbed a Coke and some jambalaya provided by the race's sponsors. Only in south Louisiana do you get jambalaya at the end of a race. We were about to head back to our hotel when I felt we ought to wait for the awards to be given.

The sponsors began with awards for the overall winners. They then went to the age divisions. Mine was 60- to 64-year-olds. Tex was talking on the phone with our daughter, Renee, who had called to see if I finished, when they announced the winner of my division. While they were talking, the announcer said, "And second place for the 60- to 64-year-olds goes to Sammy Tippit from San Antonio, Texas." Tex looked at me in surprise. Our daughter heard the announcement over Tex's cell phone. They were shocked. As I accepted the small ribbon, I could barely hold back the tears.

When we returned to our hotel room, I couldn't hold it in any longer. Tex was so sweet. She had purchased a little trophy for finishing the race and gave it to me. I had the trophy from Tex for finishing, the medal for finishing, and the ribbon for second place. I began weeping. "Honey, I don't know if you can understand how much this means to me. It's more than finishing the race," I said through my tears. "God has proven that His Word is true. He promised that if I waited on Him, He would renew my strength. I would run and not be weary. His Word is true. It's so true." Faith rested in my heart.

I knew I could now train to run the marathon in Greece. More than that, I learned the first great biblical truth about finishing the race: We run well when we wait on Him.

It's also true in the Christian life. Those who run well in the race of life are those who learn to wait for the Lord. I had learned the first principle about running with endurance: Wait to run. I was fascinated by this unique experiment. I knew one thing. I was a wounded deer who desperately needed to drink daily from the waters. As I drank from those waters, God renewed me and gave me strength. The impossible suddenly became possible.

God birthed a dream in my heart, and then He allowed circumstances into my life that would prepare me to learn a great biblical truth about running and about life. Champions wait for the Lord, and then they run. That simple truth produces unbelievable success.

---

1. Michael Perry, "The Power and the Glory," *Runner's World*, July 23, 2008, http://www.runnersworld.com/article/0,7120,s6-239-473--12789-6-1X2X3X4X5X6-7,00.html (accessed November 29, 2010).

the training

training to win

Athletes would come to me and say, "I'm not getting enough playing time. I think I should be starting. Give me a chance on Saturday to show you what I can do." I tell them, "No. That's not the way it works. You show me what you can do at practice, and I'll show the world what you can do on Saturday."
Jerry Stovall, former LSU head football coach

Now all discipline seems painful at the time, not joyful. But later it produces the fruit of peace and righteousness for those trained by it.
Hebrews 12:11

The greatest temptation for the gifted athlete is to pursue instant success rather than long-term fulfillment of a dream. In the same manner, winners in the Christian life take a long-term view of life. They see beyond short-term accolades, fortune, and fame. Their eyes are fixed on the final prize: hearing Jesus say, "Well done, good and faithful servant." Their goal is to become like Christ. They realize the prize comes to those who spend years training in Christlike character and growing in their faith.

Many great runners have taken this long-term view of success. Sebastian Coe, considered one of the greatest 800 meter and 1500 meter runners in history, had an unusual coach—his father. Sebastian Coe wrote a tribute to him and described the importance his father placed on long-term success:

> Few in their early teens have the self-awareness to be able to take the long-term view of their needs; they don't always see over the brow of the next hill. A good coach, like any good leader, needs to fire the imagination, to paint a picture of what might be there, where for some only a blank canvas exists. My coach wanted that picture to become so familiar that it became part of who we were and what we expected to achieve.[1]

Much of the greatness of Sebastian Coe can be attributed to his father's ability to paint a portrait of a dream and impart a long-term view of pursuing that dream.

That's precisely the need in our Christian lives. We desperately need God to paint a picture in our hearts of the ultimate goal: Christlike character. We must become so focused on that goal that it becomes a part of who we are and all we do. All of our daily training must point that direction, no matter how attractive a short-term goal may be. Our primary focus must always be the long-term dream, even if the short-term goal is God-given. When God gives a dream, we must also prioritize the goals He's given.

KEEPING OUR FOCUS

Focus holds the key to any kind of success. In an interview with Jerry Stovall, he kept using the word *focus*. Recently inducted to the College Hall of Fame, Coach Stovall was runner-up for the Heisman Trophy in 1962, played in three Pro Bowls, and was a two-time All Pro. All that took place before he became head coach at one of the great football powerhouses: LSU. To discover the source of Coach Stovall's success, I probed him about secrets of champions. He kept coming back to two terms: *focus* and *hard work*.

By maintaining focus on our ultimate goal, we can handle the rigors of discipline that come in daily training regimens. Lose focus and you lose the ability to face the tough times. Coach Stovall, who became a committed follower of Jesus while playing football at LSU, compared focus and hard work on the football field to daily obedience to Jesus and growing in our faith. Christlike character must remain in the forefront of our minds and hearts.

Perhaps that is why the author of Hebrews speaks of us "keeping our eyes fixed on Jesus" (Hebrews 12:2). Our focus must be Jesus. It's so easy in the Christian life to become distracted with many good things, perhaps even godly things. But if we lose focus on Who it's all about, we'll never run like champions. We begin the race by looking to Jesus, continue by looking to Him, and finish by looking to Him. All through the race, He is our focus. It's Jesus—not our programs, our methods, or our ministries. We look to Jesus, and everything in life creates character in us.

The dream of becoming like Jesus establishes our goals, and we build our priorities on those goals. If we lose sight of the dream, we may one day find ourselves placing importance on the wrong things. That can easily produce injury or even cause us to run down the wrong path. One day, we may realize we're on a road that led us far from our final destination.

CHAMPIONS PRACTICE THE BASICS

When God spoke to my heart about running, I had no idea where to begin. Thirty years earlier, my friend Ken Leeburg planned our training routine. I simply did whatever Ken outlined. After my cancer surgery, I knew I needed help with training. I went to a local bookstore and scoured the books about marathon training. One stood out: *Brain Training for Runners* by Matt Fitzgerald. As a sports physiologist, he developed a training program using scientific data.

As I read Fitzgerald's book, one simple principle gripped my heart. *The basics are basic.* Champions regularly practice the basics until they become second nature. Once the basics are so engrained that they become a natural part of their regimen, champions see improvements that enable them to do extraordinary things.

LEVELS OF TRAINING

Almost everything in Fitzgerald's system depends on four levels of training: *Base, Build I, Build II, and Peak.* You can't achieve peak performance until you master the *Base* and *Build* levels. As I methodically practiced each level of training and then progressed to another, I experienced incredible improvements in strength, endurance, and speed.

One problem Christians face is that we often place unreasonable expectations on the new believer. When I became pastor of the American military church in Germany, I noticed people were great at talking about the things of God—but most had never mastered the basics of Christian living. Many attempted to run their race at peak performance, but few had trained at the *Base* level. So I began basic discipleship training with men, and my wife did the same with women. We watched people as they began to run at their full potential.

Most of the men and women who participated became leaders in our church. When they were transferred to other areas of the world or returned to the United States, they immediately became leaders in their churches. People were often amazed at their spiritual maturity. They didn't have any great secrets that produced championship lives; they simply learned and practiced the basics.

Don Shelton was one of those men. When Don first came to our church, the only thing he had done in church was serve as an usher. But as he practiced the basics of Christian living, he became a discipleship leader and deacon. When I returned to the U.S., Don retired from the military and became pastor of the church. Several years later, I was in the lobby of a hotel in Nairobi, Kenya, and spotted Don in front of the hotel. I hadn't seen him in years. We renewed our fellowship, and I learned he was a pastor in the Dallas area and that his church was ministering to about 200 churches in East Africa. Don was running like a champion.

I recalled how, many years earlier in Germany, he was so faithful to learn and practice the basics of the Christian life. Don wasn't unique. Many of those men and women from the church in Germany ran like champions because they spent time practicing the basics of the Christian life.

Practice is the key word that transforms principles of Christian living into character in the Christian life. There's a great difference between *teaching truths* and *training in the basics*. Many Christians do well in filling out notebooks with biblical truths. But few seem willing to apply those truths. When I read Fitzgerald's book, I saw its purpose wasn't to give the reader a greater knowledge about running a marathon, although it did that. Its purpose was to enable the reader to learn and apply the principles so he or she could run a marathon at full potential. Many Christians study the Bible just to gain more knowledge. When we begin to practice the basics of Christian living, we become stronger, build endurance, and develop character.

THE BASICS OF THE CHAMPION

There are four basics of Christian living we need to apply daily if we are to become champions in life.

Listen to God

God longs to have an intimate relationship with us. He wants to communicate the deep things on His heart. How does He do that? Through His Word. The Bible is called *The Word of God* for good reason. God breathed the things on His heart into some of the great champions of the past. They wrote them down, and we know this collection of writings as the Bible. Those words speak of His character, deeds, and testimonies. When we read the Scriptures, the God who created the universe actually speaks to us. Think about that. The God who hung the stars in space is ready to reveal His plan and His character to you and me. Incredible.

Read the Bible regularly. Even if it's only a few minutes each day, spend time reading His Word. Read it devotionally. Read it with your heart, not just your mind. Read it with an attitude that says, "What do you want to say to me today?" Read it systematically. Don't just skip around the Bible. Read through entire books or study some of the Bible personalities, like Moses, Esther, David, or Paul. Read it and discover Jesus on every page. The Bible, more than any other book, will keep your gaze fixed on Jesus.

Speak to God

He not only wants to speak to you, but He also longs for you to share your heart with Him. Communication is a two-way street. Prayer is the communion of two hearts: the heart of God and your heart. One of the great discoveries in my Christian life is that I can tell God anything—and everything. I can pour out my heart to Him. I shout for joy about my victories, and He smiles. I tell Him my sorrows, and He weeps. I confess my failures, and He pours forth His grace. I share my inadequacies, and He gives strength. There is nothing I need to hide from Him. I need only to be honest and tell Him everything on my heart.

Speaking to God—and allowing God to speak to us—are basics that enrich our walk with Him. They stand as the basics for training in holiness. There's certainly more to holiness than those two disciplines, but they are foundational. When I first came to Christ, I practiced those two things, and they set the direction for my future. Three friends and I began meeting to memorize and read the Bible. We prayed together and sought God's face. People often ask me about my growth in Christ. It began with the *Base* phase. At that time my prayer life and understanding of the Bible were not close to what they are today. As I learned the basics and practiced them, God's Spirit enabled me to grow to a new level of intimacy with Him.

Listening to God and speaking to God are basic to developing holiness. But there's another part of the pursuit of the Christian life: to "pursue peace with everyone" (Hebrews 12:14). There are two very basic things we must do to pursue peace with everyone.

Build strong relationships with other Christians

When I came to know Christ, three guys helped me to grow in my faith: Fred, Don, and Charlie. We had just graduated from the same high school, and we continually challenged and encouraged each other. We became involved in local churches that taught the Bible and took an interest in our spiritual growth. Forty-five years later, all of us are not only walking with Christ but also serving Him in a significant way. We understood early in our Christian lives that we needed each other.

Many Christians become disillusioned with the church because they see so many defeated Christians. We must realize we're all on the same journey of growing into the image of Jesus. None of us has arrived.

Many years ago, I was speaking in a church in Florida. The pastor showed me around town. In the process, he took me by many of the local churches and described their ministry. We passed by one very small church. The building was so small, it appeared large enough for only one or two people. He said, "That church was begun by a man who didn't like any of the churches in town. He visited every church and came to the conclusion they were all filled with hypocrites. So he decided to build a church that was big enough for only him." I thought, *If he was honest, he would realize his little church was also filled with a hypocrite.* Only one person has ever lived the Christian life exactly as it was intended: Jesus.

When I interviewed Ryan Hall, I asked about the importance of a support group. "It's huge having a support crew and having people out on the race course supporting me," he said. "You can run a marathon any day you want to in practice. What makes it special is sharing that with other people, sharing the experience with other guys you're running with, with the crowd, and that's when you're able to test what's inside of you and push yourself to levels that you didn't even think possible. But you can't do it on your own."

If you want to run like a champion, you need to run with other Christians. Learn from them. Grow with them. Each of us is headed toward the same finish line. Some will run better than others. That's not what's important. It's the finish line that matters.

Pursue peace with those who are outside a relationship with Christ

Therefore, we need to "pursue peace" with all our brothers and sisters in Christ. But it's not only Christians with whom we're to pursue peace. It's with "everyone." That means those who are not Christians. There are two ways we can practice this principle. First, people find peace with each other when they find peace with God. When we live reconciled to God, we are given the message of reconciliation and become ambassadors for Christ. One of the greatest joys we experience as followers of Jesus is helping others enter a personal relationship with Him.

Several years ago, a terrible tragedy devastated Rwanda. Nearly one million people were killed because of their ethnic background. I traveled to the country a few months after the genocide. It was one of the most agonizing experiences of my life. I proclaimed the good news of God's love found in Jesus—and many people were reconciled not only with God but also with people from the opposing tribe. People in neighboring Burundi heard about what happened in Rwanda and sent messengers asking me to come to their country.

I agreed, but there was a major problem. Tribal factions were still at war. It was very dangerous to travel to the capital city, Bujumbura. But we hired a pilot who was willing to take the risk. A colleague, Mike Scalf, and my wife and I flew into Burundi at the height of the war. I proclaimed the wonderful love of God and invited people to give their hearts to Christ. Nearly 8,000 people—from both warring factions—responded to the invitation. Thousands came to the platform where I spoke. They knelt, prayed, and opened their hearts to Jesus.

The top story on the Bujumbura evening news was about Hutus and Tutsis praying together. The head of the government's peace negotiating team had just returned to the country from a round of negotiations. He turned on the television to see how the news covered the negotiations only to discover the lead story was about our meetings in the stadium. He immediately called and asked to meet with us.

"We've been trying for months to bring the two factions to-gether," he said. "How did you do this?"

I told him that I couldn't do it, but that the hope for peace in his country could be found in the message of the cross of Christ. Jesus' love and forgiveness had the power to change hate into love and transform bitterness into forgiveness.

He responded by saying, "This message needs to go to every person in our country."

The message of peace with God through faith in Christ had the power to bring peace to an entire nation.

There is also a second way we can pursue peace with those who don't know Christ. We must attempt to show kindness and love to those who have never experienced His grace. We need to live in such a way that the people in our communities see Christ in us. Go to the poor, the hurting, the sick, and the lonely. Show them God's love. We must go to our enemies and reach out with the grace of God. If we fail them, ask their forgiveness. If they fail us, show them His grace. Above all, pursue peace with them. That doesn't mean compromise. It means displaying Christlike attitudes of grace and love.

If we practice these basic truths, we'll learn how to run like champions. Start with these principles and build on them. There's much more to the race, but practice these simple truths all through your training—and especially in the *Base* phase. You'll become like Jesus.

LEARNING YOUR PACE

A runner doesn't become a champion overnight, and a Christian doesn't become a spiritual giant after a moment of spiritual ecstasy. We begin weak and grow strong. We start slow and develop speed. At first we tire easily, but over time we build endurance. As we identify the pace at which we can run comfortably, our strength increases, endurance emerges, and speed develops. We grow by God's grace and in His time.

One of the most critical principles of training is to identify the pace at which you can run—and practice running that pace until you become stronger and better. It's difficult because we often hold an unrealistic view of our strength and endurance. If you don't identify your level of fitness, you'll never be able to grow in strength and build enough endurance to become the person God intends.

When I began training for the Athens Classic Marathon, I needed to know the pace at which I could realistically train. Fitzgerald recommends the runner compete in a race to make that determination. He produced a formula that gives the runner an idea of his beginning training pace based on the time results of the race.

There was a series of fun runs in a park near where I live. I decided to run in one or more of those to identify my pace. There were three basic runs: half mile, mile, and five kilometers (3.1 miles). I decided to try them all. The first race was the half mile. It wasn't on a track but a road. I lined up with the rest of the participants and quickly discovered I was different from the rest of the runners. High school cross-country runners and seasoned marathoners gathered at the starting line. Then there was me, a 63-year-old, out-of-shape, overweight man, just beginning to train.

Once the starter yelled "go," something strange happened. The young thoroughbreds and the veterans lagged way behind me. At first I thought, *I must be in better shape than I thought.* At 200 meters, one-fourth of the way to the finish line, I looked back to see where everyone else was. I had a really good lead. At 300 meters, I was so far ahead of everyone, I couldn't see them. Then a terrible thought filled my mind: *There's something wrong with this picture.*

I discovered the flaw at 400 meters. It felt like rigor mortis flooding my joints and muscles. Everything moved in slow motion. My arms felt like they were carrying a 1,000-pound weight. My legs seemed frozen. Then everyone passed me—one by one, until I was nearly last! I learned a great lesson that day: the importance of pace.

Probably the most important lesson I learned about training was that the greatest improvements come in small increments. If we exercise patience in our walk with God, we can see tremendous increases in Christlike character. Change begins in one moment—the instant we come to Christ. The power for transformation takes place immediately. But character develops over a lifetime.

Too many people become discouraged because they don't see the immediate improvement they anticipated when they gave their hearts to Christ. Practice the basic principles of walk-ing with God every day, and you will look back in a year or two and be amazed at your growth.

God will provide everything you need. He will renew your strength and revive your heart. Revival often comes when we move from one phase of the race to the next. God empowers us to move to a new level in the race.

---

1. "Sebastian Coe: My Tribute to My Father, My Coach," *The Telegraph*, April 4, 2009, http://www.telegraph.co.uk/sport/othersports/olympics/london2012 /5106304/ Sebastian-Coe-my-tribute-to-my-father-my-coach.html (accessed November 29, 2010).

running hills

All available evidence suggests that "mentally tough" runners accept race pain—to the point of even welcoming and embracing it—more than other runners, and that this acceptance enables them to run harder.

The meaning of "accepting pain" is quite literal. When it comes, you don't wish it away, but instead welcome it as an indication that you are working as hard as you should be.[1]

Matt Fitzgerald in Brain Training for Runners

My aim is to know him, to experience the power of his resurrection, to share in his sufferings, and to be like him in his death.

Philippians 3:10

When the Bible uses the word *hills*, that carries few implications for the average reader. Not for the runner. When someone in our culture faces a hill, he or she normally sees it through an automobile windshield. The average person doesn't even notice hills when riding in a car. Just a little push of the pedal, and you're up. No big deal. But the runner sees it differently. As a runner, everything changes when you see a hill. Your stride and pace change. You prepare for a different level of difficulty and effort. Your body takes a different posture. Your breathing rate increases.

Most people read Psalm 121:1–2 and receive spiritual insight: "I look up toward the hills. From where does my help come? My help comes from the Lord, the Creator of heaven and earth!" The reader may see the beauty, power, and majesty of God's creation and be reminded of a great spiritual truth about God as Creator. The runner sees the same thing—but also reads these verses with a very practical application.

Our ministry co-sponsored a conference at the Billy Graham Training Center, The Cove, in North Carolina's Blue Ridge Mountains. Located at the top of a small mountain, The Cove has a spectacular view. When my wife and I arrived at the gated entrance, a sense of anticipation overtook us. We knew a beautiful building with an incredible view sat at the top of the hill. Excitement filled our hearts as we drove up the hill and prepared for an awesome time of worship and study.

But when a runner stands near that entrance and prepares to ascend the hill, he sees something altogether different. He looks up that steep hill and begins quoting Psalm 121: "I look up toward the hills. From where does my help come?" He sees difficulty rather than beauty. His heart begins to palpitate. Sweat breaks out. A sense of dread and fear overtake him. It becomes a very practical question. Where will the runner find the strength to make it up the mountain? The psalmist says, "My help comes from the Lord." For the runner, the trip up that hill becomes an act of faith.

A runner sees that verse much differently than someone who drives up the hill. Both insights into that passage are valid. But for the runner, hills hold difficulties as well as beauty. Thousands of years ago, most people probably had a similar view. They had to walk up hills, often carrying heavy loads. Like today's runner, they knew they needed God to strengthen them. At a distance, the hills displayed God's glory. But up close, those same hills produced a sense of need for God.

Reading the Bible through the eyes of the athlete gives us fresh insight into the needs of the Christian. God often sends the greatest seasons of revival when we face insurmountable hills. How we see those difficulties may determine our future strength, endurance, and character.

Renewal normally happens as we face difficulties. We often think of revival as a mountaintop experience. But I've seen a greater work of God while climbing hills than while resting at the top. The struggle causes me to call on God for His strength. I develop more character while climbing hills than at any other time in my Christian life.

That was one of the first lessons I learned when I ran with Ken Leeburg. Ken came to me after a service in Germany one Sunday and said, "I hear you're a runner." When I responded positively, he said, "Great. Let's meet on Saturday and run together."

Ken had a very steep hill he liked to run. Though it was thirty years ago, it seems I can still hear Ken's voice shouting and encouraging me to conquer the hill. I didn't know it then, but Ken was teaching me the fundamentals of the truths found in Hebrews 12.

Later that year, we ran a half marathon before we both returned to the United States. After coming home, we kept in close contact and informed each other of our workouts. We were still working toward running the Athens Marathon. Then one day a shocking phone call came. A mutual friend said, "Sammy, sit down. I have some terrible news. Ken was just killed in an automobile accident."

I sat stunned. Ken was so young and strong. It was hard to believe. I sat in silence for what seemed a lifetime. Tex saw me and asked, "What's wrong?"

I groaned, "Oh, God." Then more silence. I stammered through telling her what I had just heard.

After talking to my wife about the conversation, we called Ken's wife, Lyn. She asked me to preach at the memorial service. Tex and I immediately went to be with Lyn. My heart ached so badly. It was the first time in my life to lose a best friend in a tragic accident. It wouldn't be the last.

As I sat on the platform looking at those assembled in the military chapel, a sick feeling rose in my stomach. *How could I comfort them when I desperately needed consolation?* The answer came through Ken's children. Right before I spoke, his four daughters sang a song we'd learned at our church in Germany. It was his favorite Scripture chorus. Tears ran down my cheeks as they sang "Our God Reigns."

That song held the first biblical truth I needed to face the tragedy. I needed to know deep in my heart that God was in control—no matter how difficult the situation. I didn't know it then, but God was building character.

I asked God for the strength to speak. As courage rose in my heart, I told the audience, "Ken used to run hills in Germany. One of the hills was so long and so difficult, I named it Difficulty.

Today, Ken has left us the most difficult hill in life to climb. This hill is surely called Difficulty. He's in heaven cheering us on, telling us to never give up—that we can overcome it."

At that time, I didn't understand the importance of running hills. But God was preparing me for the race. He was teaching me to embrace the hills in life. I didn't grasp what was happening, but God was transforming me inwardly. He was building strength and endurance through the difficult events. Revival was occurring in the secret place. I was learning that Christlike character is more often developed climbing hills than standing on mountaintops. The hills looked like great burdens. But they were really my friends. That made sense only as I thought about the song Ken's daughters sang at his funeral: "Our God Reigns."

EMBRACING THE HILLS

Difficulties. God's sovereignty. Faith. They create strength and endurance. In a mysterious way, the hill of difficulty created a hunger and thirst to become more like Christ. I learned to embrace my difficulties rather than fight them. The seeds of personal revival were planted on a hill called Difficulty.

The author of Hebrews tells us to "run with endurance the race set out for us" (12:1) He then exhorts us to "[keep] our eyes fixed on Jesus" (12:2). That statement is followed with, "Think of him who endured such opposition against himself by sinners, so that you may not grow weary in your souls and give up" (12:3). The passage then speaks of the *resistance* we face. The next eight verses use the word *discipline* to describe how we train in righteousness. The hills of life are God's resistance training that increases our spiritual strength.

Hills will always be a part of our lives. We can run away from them, fight them, or embrace them. Jesus embraced the cross as His ultimate purpose for coming to earth. When we consider Him and the hill He climbed, we stand amazed at His strength and endurance. No one has ever climbed a hill like the one He climbed. He displayed the immeasurable strength of God on that hill.

He is our example. When we understand God's ultimate purpose for hills, we embrace them and run like champions. Many fail to become champions because they never learn to embrace the hills of life. Difficulties come and go. They feel the pain and fight it. They suffer sorrows, and their experience produces no positive results. They grow tired and lose heart. As one author wrote many years ago, "They waste their sorrows."

That's what happened to the Hebrew believers. That's why the book was written: to remind them of the One Who climbed the most difficult hill in history, a hill called Golgotha. It was the hill from which God's glory radiated as never before. More was accomplished on that hill to help mankind than in all the schools throughout history. More strength and character flowed from that hill than from all the political capitals that ever existed. That hill became the source of God's glory, character, and spiritual strength to all who look to the One Who climbed it.

None of us has ever been asked to climb a hill like that one. By comparison, the hills God gives us to climb are small. When we embrace them, we grow stronger. We become more like the

One Who climbed Golgotha. We see the One True Champion, and we know we've been given the privilege to follow in His footsteps.

I learned about the strength that comes from running hills after I ran in the San Antonio Senior Games. I was looking forward to running the 400 meters there because I ran that distance in high school. But I did very poorly. There was one critical training regimen that helped me improve greatly: running hills.

One of my competitors in San Antonio was a longtime friend and my accountant, Tom Flournoy. When I checked the times from previous years, I saw Tom had the best record for my age division and would probably win the race. Still, I felt confident I could stay close to him most of the race. Once the gun went off and we rounded the first curve, Tom passed me. *This isn't supposed to be happening,* I thought. *He should be passing me in the second curve. I must be running very slowly.* When the race was over, Tom won just as I expected. Yet my time was also about what I anticipated. Tom had improved drastically.

After congratulating him, I said, "I saw your previous times on the Internet. How did you improve so much?"

He said, "Let me introduce you to my friend, Julio." After introducing me, he told me Julio had been training him. He credited most of his success to Julio's training.

Then Julio asked, "Would you like to train with us?"

"That would be fantastic," I said.

"Meet us Thursday morning at Brackenridge Park."

I met Tom and Julio not knowing what kind of workout to expect.

Julio told us, "Guys, we need to go back to the basics—build strength and stamina. We'll do hill work today." We walked for a mile—then jogged a mile.

At that point, I thought, *This is a piece of cake.* We ended our jog at the bottom of a hill and Julio said, "We're going to run this hill. But Sammy, I know guys like you. You'll try to sprint it. Don't do that. Let me pace both of you. Stay right by my side."

I did what he said, and we ran up the hill at a steady but not too difficult pace. Just when I thought we were at the top, the hill turned and kept going. It happened one more time. At the top, I was winded but handled it pretty well. "How did that feel?" Julio said.

"Great."

"Okay, let's go down the hill."

I felt decent. It didn't hurt nearly as much as I anticipated. At the bottom of the hill, Julio asked, "Are you ready?"

"For what?" I said.

"To run back up the hill."

"Sure." We took off with the same pace. This time I was more than winded. My lungs began to burn and my legs tire.

"Are you okay?" Julio asked. I said yes, and Julio took us back down the hill.

"That was a good workout," I told Julio.

With a sly smile he said, "It's not over. We're going back up the hill."

My face fell. "You're kidding."

"No. Let's go."

This time my quads began burning before the first turn. When we finished, I bent in agony trying to catch my breath. Once I returned to normalcy, Julio directed us down the hill. We ran the hill six times! Before we started the sixth rep, Julio chuckled. "I love to run hills," he said. "They make you strong."

Hill training became a vital part of our *Base* workouts. A few months later, when I ran in the state championships and won, the guy who came in third place approached me. "Where did you come from?" he said. "I've never seen you in any of the races."

I told him this was my first state championship, and I had run only one other time in Texas. "I ran in San Antonio a few months ago."

"No," he shot back. "I ran in San Antonio and came in second place. I didn't see you."

"I know," I said. "I was so far behind, you would never have seen me. I came in second to last place."

"Wow! How did you improve so quickly?"

With a smile, I said, "Let me introduce you to Julio. He loves to run hills!"

RESISTANCE TRAINING

Among runners, hill training is synonymous with strength training. Both are forms of resistance training. There are two primary ways for the runner to practice resistance training: with weights or hill training. But hill training allows the runner to build strength in a more natural manner. The muscles the athlete uses during a race are being strengthened while performing race-specific movements.

Arthur Lydiard is one of the greatest middle and long distance coaches of all time. He coached many of the greats and has been asked to help around the world with his system of training. From Finland to Russia, East Germany, Mexico, Denmark, Venezuela, and the United States, Lydiard popularized his training method. He notes that "running up hills forces you to lift the knees higher. This is one of the most desirable developments for any runner, as this governs stride speed and length. It also develops the muscles fibers, thus increasing power."[2] When the runner practices hill training, he or she almost always returns to the track much faster and stronger.

God wants us to run like champions. Without His resistance training, we don't develop the strength to run to our full potential. He allows us to face hills called Difficulty so He can make us strong. When we meet others in the race, they may wonder how we had the power to change. They may ask us what caused us to improve so much.

With a smile we can tell them, "I love to run hills. They make you strong."

---

1. Matt Fitzgerald, *Brain Training for Runners* (New York: New American Library, 2007) 157.

2. Arthur Lydiard with Garth Gilmour, *Running the Lydiard Way* (Mountain View, California: World Publications, 1978) 52.

strengthening your weaknesses

When Felix Limo does a half-marathon practice run to see what his weak parts are, he is seeking critical feedback to correct weakness.[1]
from "Sweaty Secrets of Kenya's Running Factory"

Therefore, strengthen your listless hands and your weak knees.
Hebrews 12:12

The greatest long distance runners in the world come from Kenya. It hasn't always been that way. Wilson Kiprugut won Kenya's first gold medal during the 1964 Olympic Games in Tokyo. After he won the 800 meters, Kenya saw a boom in racing. At the 1968 Olympics in Mexico, Kenyans won eleven medals. Since then, Kenyans have dominated the international long distance racing scene.

Most of the great long distance runners come from not just Kenya but one particular area of Kenya. Most hail from the Kerio Valley. Training camps have sprung up around Eldoret, an agricultural city there. Physiologists have studied the Kenyans and written books about them. Coaches have observed the patterns, habits, and training methods of the Kenyan runners. Everyone wants to know, "What makes the Kenyans so great? Is it their DNA, food, or type of training?" The world has been mystified at the Kenyans' success.

I asked Ryan Hall, who made an interesting observation. "It's easily accessible," he said. "Everyone can do it. Kids grow up being inspired by these elite runners who can do amazing things. It creates a lot of interest and gets a lot of talent out there. They have a big pool of kids to draw from, and they are running a ton of mileage at a very young age. I think one of the biggest things is that in their culture it's seen as something fun."

It's also a way to escape poverty. European and North American race promoters want Kenyans in their races and are willing to pay substantial sums to have them. Even mid-level athletes are sought out. When I ran the Athens Classic Marathon, four of the top five finishers were Kenyans. Many Kenyan runners spend up to four months a year racing in Europe or North America. A successful tour can enable a runner to escape poverty and begin a new life.

Kenyans lead the pack in the *Athens Classic Marathon.*

But money isn't the only motivation. One of Kenya's greatest, Felix Limo, won the Chicago Marathon in 2005 and 2006. He also won the London Marathon in 2006. Yet he races outside the country only four weeks a year. He spends the rest of his time in Kenya training. He doesn't race primarily for the money. He runs to identify his weaknesses and correct them. He said, "I normally call this half-marathon a tune-up race. I have to go see ... test. I go there one month before the race [marathon]; when I come back, I have to evaluate. Where was my weak part? Was it endurance? Was it speed? So I have to work on my weak part."[2] Limo wants to identify his weaknesses so he can correct them before the major championships.

Limo's perspective differs greatly from that of much Christian literature. Many Christians focus on their strengths—and neglect their weaknesses. Yet one of the world's greatest long distance runners commits himself to identifying and correcting his weakness so he can run like a champion. When we read Hebrews 12, we find a similar perspective. The author says, "Strengthen your listless hands and your weak knees." The Bible points to the believer's weakness and exhorts us to strengthen it.

WEAKNESSES ARE DIFFICULT TO RECOGNIZE

One reason we don't deal with weaknesses in our life is that they're often hard for us to identify. Others see our weaknesses more easily than we can. For me, learning that lesson proved costly. After winning the 400 meters at the Texas Senior Games, I was pumped about the future. I felt I had plenty of room for improvement because I won Texas after only a couple of months of training for that event.

"Sammy, don't you have problems with your knees?" friends often asked. "You're over 60, and your knees don't bother you?"

I always replied quickly, "No. God has really blessed me. My knees have never been a problem." It was a foolish answer.

One day, I was 20 seconds from completing a workout when I heard a loud pop, and I dropped to the ground in agony. The injury to my knee kept me from running for five months. After an MRI test and a visit with an orthopedic surgeon, I learned my injury had probably been in the works for years. Not only did I have osteoarthritis, but I also had a torn meniscus, a Baker's cyst, and inflammation. The latter three were caused by the osteoarthritis, which had been hiding inside my knee for a long time.

I should have known there was a problem, but I ignored the symptoms. Occasionally as I trained, my right knee would give. It didn't hurt. There was only a momentary weakness as I ran. Though it happened fairly consistently, I felt no pain. So I concluded I didn't have a problem.

That seems to be the way many of us run the race God gives us. As long as we don't experience pain, we assume we're okay. We don't take time to identify our weaknesses—though we all have some. Everyone has blind spots. They remain hidden for years. Then at an unsuspecting moment, we collapse because we never dealt with our weakness.

IDENTIFY YOUR WEAKNESSES

It's critical that we learn to identify our weaknesses—and deal with them in an appropriate manner. If we're going to run like champions, we must know our vulnerabilities and do everything to strengthen those areas of our lives.

If one of the world's greatest runners needs to identify his weakness to win the world championship, how much more do we need to identify our weaknesses if we're to run our race as Christ's champions?

The heart attitude we most need so we can identify our weaknesses is humility. When I interviewed Ryan Hall, I asked about his greatest struggle as an athlete. He spoke of the battle he faces between pride and humility. "I'm so inspired by Moses, the most humble man to walk the earth," he said. "I want to walk in his steps."

It takes considerable humility to make a serious effort to identify our weaknesses. We like to be told how great we are and want others to see our strengths but seldom want anyone to know our weaknesses. Yet recognizing our weaknesses produces strength.

The apostle Paul understood this. He talked about a thorn in his flesh. But Paul learned that God made him weak so His strength would be manifested. God's grace was sufficient at the point of Paul's weakness. He said, "So then, I will boast most gladly about my weaknesses, so that the power of Christ may reside in me" (2 Corinthians 12:9). The power to run and finish the race lies in God's power—not ours. We become like Jesus, not by our diligent works or outstanding abilities, but by His power—which is most clearly seen in our weaknesses.

When we acknowledge our weaknesses, we're running on the path of humility. God's grace can be appropriated only on that race course. There's no room for His grace in a heart full of pride. So if we're to run like champions, we must develop a heart of humility that is willing to face our weaknesses.

We can learn about the humility of Moses that Ryan referred to in Numbers 12. In that passage, God says Moses was the most humble man on earth. This comment came after Moses was criticized by his own brother and sister. Instead of taking the criticism personally, Moses exercised restraint and displayed love even for those who criticized him.

A friend once said, "When I hear criticism, I try to always remember that the truth is normally worse than the criticism." Whenever he was criticized, my friend tried to see if there was any truth in it. If there was, he dealt with the concern. If not, he used the experience as a time of reflection to discover any weakness.

FOUR WAYS TO DISCERN WEAKNESSES

Although weaknesses can be difficult to discover, God has given us ways to discern them. First, *He will be faithful to speak through His Word.* If we read the Bible consistently and devotionally, the still, small voice of His Spirit will gently expose our weaknesses. It's mysterious yet remarkable how God can speak into specific areas of our lives through a Book written thousands of years ago. This is the best way because God's Word doesn't just expose our weaknesses, but it also shows us how to strengthen those areas of our lives.

Second, *others will often see our weaknesses before we see them.* When I began training, a friend showed me some drills that would improve my form. As I performed those drills, my right knee momentarily collapsed. Because it didn't hurt, I ignored it. My friend suggested I check out why that happened, but I ignored his advice. If I had listened to him I could have saved myself from injury and five months of sitting on the sidelines. It's good to have trusted friends who love you and speak honestly into your life. They often see things you overlook. Listen to the counsel of Christlike friends.

Third, *listen to your heart.* There's an interesting concept found in much athletic literature. Even with all the efforts to improve running through scientific research, some of the best scientists still say, "Listen to your body. It contains the best indicators of your fitness and training needs." That was certainly true with my knee injury. After hard workouts, I often felt soreness behind my knee. My body was telling me I had a problem—a Baker's cyst. Had I listened, I could have avoided injury.

Similarly, your heart contains the best indicators of your spiritual fitness. If you listen closely to your heart, God's Spirit will speak in the deepest part of your soul. The key word is *listen.* That's one reason waiting on God becomes so important in the Christian life. In those times of silence we most often hear the voice of God's Spirit.

There's a fourth way we can identify weaknesses, but it may be the most difficult. *Weaknesses are often exposed during conflict.* Our pursuit as a Christian is twofold: "peace with everyone, and holiness" (Hebrews 12:14). Anything that keeps us from achieving those objectives is either a hindrance or a weakness. When conflict arises, it becomes a great opportunity to ask God to search our hearts and show us our weaknesses. Perhaps that's what happened to Moses when the Bible describes him as the most humble man on earth.

TURNING WEAKNESS INTO STRENGTH

Identifying your weaknesses is only half the equation. Correcting them is the other half— and the more difficult part. It's at the point of correction that we grow and become more like Jesus. That's when we make the greatest improvements in our pursuit of holiness. For an elite runner like Felix Limo, correcting a weakness becomes a matter of directed discipline. He identifies his weakness and then develops specific training strategies to overcome it. He disciplines himself accordingly so he runs at full potential.

In our pursuit as Christians, there are some similarities to the athlete's approach to weakness, but there is one major difference. The athlete's success largely depends on his willpower. But the Christian's victory requires the supernatural grace of God. The athlete receives honor for overcoming weakness, but the Christian gives all glory to God.

The most poignant passage in the Bible concerning weakness comes from the apostle Paul in 2 Corinthians 12. When God refused Paul's request to remove the thorn in his flesh, he was placed in a position to listen to what God was saying. Paul probably struggled with pride. He had witnessed God work many miracles through his life and ministry and had experienced deep encounters with Christ. But Paul knew it was easy to develop a type of spiritual arrogance that grows in the soil of success.

Two decisions and one supernatural work of God's Spirit produced in Paul an attitude of faith that turned his weakness into strength. First, Paul chose not to boast about his strengths but rather his weaknesses. He knew that the glory of God was more clearly seen in his weaknesses than in his strengths. Paul also knew that the race wasn't about himself but about Jesus. He never wanted to forget that. So his weaknesses stood as a reminder of the great opportunity to manifest God's power and glory. Therefore, Paul determined to boast in his weaknesses rather than his strengths. Paul maintained an attitude that said, "Hey guys, I'm not a spiritual superstar. I'm just like you, a person with weaknesses. So, don't glorify me. All the glory belongs to Jesus."

Second, Paul chose contentment over frustration during times of weakness. When he faced insults, problems, and persecution, he allowed God to display His grace. He understood that God sits on His throne. He's in control. When faced with opposition, difficulties, and rejection, Paul refused to succumb to discouragement. He saw God's hand as well as an opportunity to grow in God's grace. He refused to give in to life's irritations but rather chose to bask in the goodness and grace of God.

Besides making these two key decisions that put him on the path to victory, Paul also exercised simple faith. God spoke deeply to his heart, saying, "My grace is enough for you, for my power is made perfect in weakness" (2 Corinthians 12:9). Paul's greatness could be attributed to only the grace and power of God. He appropriated God's power by faith. That's the way the men and women of old ran their race—and the way Paul chose to run his.

Early in my Christian life, I discovered this great truth. God gave me victory over many weaknesses as a new believer, but I continued to struggle with some deep-seated vulnerabilities. I wanted victory but failed consistently. I didn't know how to overcome them. The harder I tried to defeat those attitudes and habits, the bigger they became. When I realized that I couldn't overcome them, I looked to Jesus—and His strength enabled me to overcome. I brought those areas of my life to Him daily and trusted Jesus to live victoriously through me. I found victory, but I could only say it was by God's strength, not mine.

Weaknesses expose our neediness. We cry to God when we see how needy we really are. When our hearts cry to God, we come to know His heart. When we see His heart, we see grace, astounding grace. That grace reminds us we are "wounded deer" in need of God's resources. Our need causes us to drink from His streams of living water. The waters that flow from His throne fill us with fresh power to run the race and become like Christ.

Felix Limo understood he had weaknesses, but he learned to identify and deal with them. It made him a champion. God wants us to live as champions. When we're willing to recognize and admit our weaknesses, we're training in righteousness. God then comes to our rescue and empowers us to overcome. We can then say with the apostle Paul, "We have complete victory through him who loved us!" (Romans 8:37). We run like champions.

---

1. Jackie Lebo, "Sweaty Secrets of Kenya's Running Factory," *East Africa Magazine*, August 11–17, 2008, III.

2. Ibid., II.

healing injuries

When my name was called, I stepped on top of the podium and they placed the gold medal around my neck. I felt like I was dreaming. ... Standing on the podium with the gold medal draped around my neck was very emotional for me. ... I was overwhelmed with happiness.[1]

Charles Austin, gold medalist in high jump in the 1996 Olympic Games

And make straight paths for your feet, so that what is lame may not be put out of joint but be healed.

Hebrews 12:13

The tension ran high in the Olympic stadium in Atlanta as Charles Austin prepared for his jump. The bar had been raised higher than anyone had ever jumped in the Olympic Games. Austin focused, took a couple of steps, accelerated, leaped—and cleared the bar. Tens of thousands of people went wild—jumping, screaming, and waving American flags. Austin bounced from the mat, thrusting his arms high.

After Austin's jump, the only person who could stand in the way of his Olympic gold was the Polish jumper. He attempted, but failed. For the first time since 1968, an American won gold in high jump. He also established a new Olympic record. Thousands in the stands and millions via television watched as Austin ran his victory lap.

Yet there was a part of the victory that most observers didn't know. Charles Austin defied the odds to become the world's champion. Three years earlier he had injured his knee, and the injury required surgery. Doctors in Texas and Europe told him he would never jump again at a championship level. "I sank to an all time low when I heard their diagnosis," Austin wrote. "They basically told me that my career was over."[2]

Then a surgeon in San Antonio performed surgery on his knee. When Austin began the rehabilitation process, he developed two attitudes that enabled him to overcome the injury. First, he made a faith decision. "I refused to believe my career was over."[3] Austin understood a great truth: Faith is much more than mental assent to a set of dogma. It's also much more than an emotional state. Along with intellectual belief and emotional desire, faith takes root in our will. We must make a choice. That may be the most difficult part of faith.

Second, Austin applied a systematic set of exercises to rehabilitate his knee. "As long as I had a one percent chance of being able to resume my high jump career," he said, "I was going to give it my all to make it happen."[4] Faith without action isn't faith at all. Faith isn't some pie-in-the-sky feeling that leaves you passive about life. Faith doesn't exist in a vacuum. It exists in the midst of hurt, pain, and injury. Faith motivates us to actions that cause us to appropriate God's power to accomplish things that seem impossible.

When the author of Hebrews wrote about the great champions of the past, he highlighted the need for faith. "Without faith it is impossible to please him, for the one who approaches God must believe that he exists and that he rewards those who seek him" (Hebrews 11:6). Such faith often arises in our hearts as we see the faith of others. That's why Hebrews 11 is critical to understanding chapter 12's exhortation to "run with endurance"— especially as it applies to injuries.

Life's most discouraging moments often accompany injuries. To the athlete, they can be debilitating. In our spiritual lives, they seem devastating. Yet when we see someone who has run the race and overcome injuries, hope rises in our hearts and we think, *If they can do it, perhaps I can also.*

That may be one of the secrets of the Kenyan runners. After one person won a medal in the Olympics, his neighbors and friends may have thought, *I know that guy. He's no different from me. If he can do this, so can I.* Every time a Kenyan runner won, more faith rose in the hearts of those in the region. An entire running industry was birthed in a nation. People began to believe, and the impossible suddenly became possible.

That's what happened in my life when I met Charles Austin on a track in San Antonio. I had no idea who he was. When he began telling me his story, I found it hard to believe I had just met the greatest high jumper in American history. As I read his story on the Internet, faith began to rise in my heart because I had also injured my knee. If he had suffered a knee injury, overcome it, and become the world's champion, then possibly I could overcome my injury—though I had not been able to work out for months. Faith births faith.

THE SOURCES OF INJURIES

There are two ways to deal with injuries: prevent them or heal them. Obviously the first method is best. To prevent injuries, we must know why they occur and where our vulnerabilities lie. Once we trace the source of our injuries, we can understand ways to prevent them. This critical information allows the athlete to run at his or her full potential.

There are four major sources of injuries: *an innate deficiency, our own wrong actions, injury inflicted by others,* and *seasons of change.* When we recognize those times in our lives, we can prepare ourselves. The preparation prevents or reduces our risk of injury.

An innate deficiency

Each of us has natural weaknesses. If we don't recognize them, we become vulnerable to injury. When I trained for the Athens Classic Marathon, I gradually built my weekly mileage. About five weeks before the marathon, I was up to 18 miles for my long Saturday run. I'll never forget that morning. After lacing my shoes, as I attempted to stand up, a sharp pain shot through my back. I fell on the floor and cried out for my wife. It took her nearly 15 minutes to help me up and get me to the bedroom. She called our chiropractor, who graciously agreed to see me that Saturday.

The doctor's x-rays exposed a defect. One of my legs was naturally shorter than the other. Having one short leg is a common condition. But while most people develop the condition because of poor posture, mine was a birth defect. Due to the amount of training I had done, my pelvis had shifted. Yet my doctor said that was good news. There were two simple fixes for the injury. First, he needed to manipulate and realign my pelvis.

Second, I needed to wear a heel lift in my shoe to cause both feet to strike the ground equally.

Because the injury seemed severe, many people thought I wouldn't be able to run the Athens Classic Marathon. But within two weeks, I resumed my training schedule with a heal lift in my shoe and no pain in my back. From that point, I purchased only running shoes with room for a heal lift. It was a simple but necessary fix. After that, I never had a problem with my back.

If we are willing to objectively evaluate our lives, we can often take simple steps to prevent serious injuries. A natural weakness doesn't have to become a major injury. But we must allow the Great Physician to x-ray our hearts and attitudes by His Spirit. As He exposes the defective areas, we're able to make the needed adjustments.

Our own wrong actions

Injuries also come through incorrect actions or attitudes. We develop life patterns that keep us from running at full potential, and they often produce injury. I asked Charles Austin about preventing and overcoming knee injuries. He said, "I work with a lot of professional athletes and everyday people who say the same thing: 'Oh my knees. I've had knee problems for 20 years. I can't do this because of my knees.' That's not necessarily true. It's about learning how to do things correctly, like keeping your feet straight. Also, you strengthen those muscles around your knee as well as keep excess weight down. The more weight you carry, the more force you apply to your knees, joints, tendons, and ligaments. You want to be very efficient with your movement as well as keeping lean muscle. Your body can then work the way it's supposed to."

I find it interesting that Austin referred to two specific actions to prevent knee injury. The author of Hebrews refers to weak knees and preventing injuries in a similar manner. When that writer said to "strengthen … your weak knees," he may not have known all the intricacies of preventing injury that Austin mentioned. But he knew there were specific actions Christians could take to prevent injuries in the race God has given us. According to Austin, we strengthen our knees when we strengthen the muscles around them. From a life perspective, we can surround our weaknesses with actions that will prevent them from causing an injury.

If a person has a weakness with lust, he needs to put a system of protection on his computer that keeps him from injuring his marriage. If a person has a problem with speaking harshly, he may need to discipline himself to hold his speech for thirty seconds before he responds in an emotionally charged conversation. We need to take actions that strengthen the weak areas in our lives.

But Austin also mentioned "keeping your feet straight." That sounds very similar to the Hebrews verse: "And make straight paths for your feet, so that what is lame may not be put out of joint" (12:13). Straight paths provide safety from injury and produce healing if we've been injured. "Foot strike" is critical to the long distance runner. The condition of the path also plays an important role in keeping the runner healthy. The more we run on surfaces full of potholes and twists, the more susceptible we are to injury. After my knee incident, I learned to run on surfaces and in places that would not worsen my injury.

In the race of life, we can avoid injury by carefully choosing the paths on which we run. Some paths are full of potholes called temptation. Others have twists and turns that are far from the straight and narrow way to which Jesus calls us. Too many of us train on surfaces that lead to injury. The young evangelist I mentioned at the beginning of this book had chosen to run on a crooked path. It led to the breakup of his marriage. All of us face choices about the paths on which we run. Stay away from paths that you know are filled with temptations leading to injury.

Injury inflicted by others

Often injuries occur because of something done to us. I've never met anyone in the race God gives us who hasn't been hurt by a fellow runner. After the author of Hebrews describes our pursuit in the race, "Pursue peace with everyone, and holiness, for without it no one will see the Lord," he issues a warning: "See to it that no one comes short of the grace of God, that no one be like a bitter root springing up and causing trouble, and through him many become defiled" (12:14–15).

When someone wrongs us, we can respond in one of two ways. We can become bitter—or we can appropriate the grace of God. If we choose the path of bitterness, we become a bitter root that has the potential to defile many others. When a Christian has been hurt, division often arises in the body of Christ. When someone within an ethnic community is injured, bitterness can spread throughout the culture. Bitterness always produces hurt and injuries.

When I went to Rwanda after the genocide, I saw the effect of bitterness on future generations. This wasn't the first time the nation had seen genocide. Deep hurts had been passed from previous generations. Old wounds had never healed, and bitterness devastated the country. In one month in 1994, nearly a million people were killed.

It doesn't have to be that way—personally or nationally. God provides a way to prevent injuries inflicted by others. Hebrews 12:15 exhorts us not to "[come] short of the grace of God." We must never forget we're allowed to run by grace. It's not by our own merit but by His grace that we run. Grace is the unmerited favor given by God. He loves us and gave His own Son to take the punishment for our sins. It's not because of anything we've done that we have been given the opportunity to run.

So when someone hurts us, we need to draw deeply from the well of grace and forgiveness that God has placed within. Often that seems impossible. But remember the words of Jesus: "What is impossible for mere humans is possible for God" (Luke 18:27). There's no limit to the grace that flows from His rivers. When you drink often from those rivers, you will have the supernatural strength to forgive—and be able to continue in the race.

I learned of this supernatural power when I spoke at the National University of Rwanda not long after the genocide. While there, I had lunch with the mayor of the city. My heart sank as he told me his story. When the order was given to kill Tutsis, his neighbor and friend (a Hutu) came to him saying, "You'll never be able to hide all seven of your children. Let me take some of them and hide them. They will be safe with me." But as soon as the neighbor had the children in his house, he called for the militia. They took the children and killed them.

I could hardly believe what I heard. "How did you handle that?" I said.

I'll never forget his response. "The hurt is so deep and the pain so real. I still feel it every day, but by God's grace, I forgave him and continue to forgive him."

His response wasn't natural; it was supernatural. It was impossible for any human to respond that way alone, but it's altogether possible when God places His grace in our hearts.

Draw deeply from God's grace and forgiveness. Bitterness will take you out of the race because you won't be able to "pursue peace with everyone." Living by God's grace serves as a protective covering for your heart and thrusts you in pursuit of peace with everyone.

Seasons of change

During times of change we become vulnerable to injury. So it's important to train with care during those seasons of life. I asked Ryan Hall about avoiding injuries. "Most injuries happen as a result of doing something new that you haven't done before," Hall said. "For example, a lot of injuries take place when you're just getting into running or after you've taken a break and you're just starting back up. It happens because you're introducing a whole bunch of different stimuli that the body's not used to dealing with. I think if you can keep things as consistent as possible the month before the marathon, it helps a lot."

His counsel was helpful when I began doing speed work. I built my mileage slowly and became accustomed to running long distances when I trained for the Athens Classic Marathon. But when I started training for Masters Track and Field, I experienced one injury after another. It took a while before I realized

I needed to try to improve my speed in small increments—just as I had done with longer, slower running. I was subjecting my body to new stimuli, and it needed time to adjust.

God brings each of us through different seasons in life. These times can bring us to heights we've never known. They can greatly advance us in our walk with God. But we must be careful during those times. Waiting on God becomes extremely important when we transition into a new season of life. As we wait on Him, our pace slows, and He enables us to handle the new activities, situations, relationships, and responsibilities.

HEALING INJURIES

Once we have been injured, how do we find healing? Faith is our first step in the healing process. Too many people believe they can never finish the race because of an injury. They give up, losing sight of the reward that awaits them. The injury festers until it becomes deadly.

If I've learned anything about the Christian life in the past forty-five years, I've learned the only way we'll finish the race is by God's grace—not by our strength and willpower. At some point in the race we all fail. We all become injured. The difference between a winner and a loser lies in a single moment of faith. The instant we choose to believe that God's grace is still available to us, the healing begins.

One of the biggest helps to my running came at the beginning—the moment God spoke to my heart and told me to run. I started from the position of being injured. That's why the "wounded deer" imagery became so important. From the start, I had to believe God's grace was sufficient to enable me to run a marathon. So when injuries came my way, they didn't stop me. Instead they became another opportunity to draw from the waters that flow from God's throne. I knew my identity: a wounded deer. I knew I was susceptible to injury and needed to drink daily from the healing waters of God's grace.

Too many of us forget who we are. We begin to think we're superstars in God's kingdom. We think we can run and never be injured. We forget we're wounded deer. When a superstar gets knocked off his pedestal, he has a hard time believing he can get back up. But a wounded deer knows he must return to the waters.

Grace is God's supernatural medicine that brings healing. Faith is the application of that medicine. Yet there's one more element to God's method of healing: time. Some people think time heals everything. I don't. Once you've been to places like Rwanda and Burundi, you know time doesn't have the power to heal. It may help us forget, but the wound remains lodged in our soul unless God supernaturally heals the hurt. God heals by grace, which is appropriated by faith. He then uses time to remove the scars.

Though time is not the healer, it plays a critical role in the process. Elite runners understand the importance of time and its place in healing injuries. Charles Austin needed surgery and had to go through rehabilitation. That provided healing. Time didn't heal him, but it was a necessary part. Though this sounds like a simple truth everyone understands, it's seldom applied. Time demands patience, and too many seem unwilling to develop it. Yet as we practice patience, we develop endurance—and endurance separates winners from losers.

One of my greatest temptations when I injured my knee was to get back on the track before I was completely healed. Fortunately, my doctor used objective observations to discern when I was ready to run again. He didn't hesitate to say, "You're not ready yet."

I've watched many wounded Christians fail to take the time to allow God to completely heal their injury. They appropriate God's grace by faith—then foolishly say, "It's done. I'm healed. Let's get back to work." Within a short time, they injure themselves again.

It sounds counterintuitive to say "God's grace is sufficient—but let's take some time for the healing process to be complete." That's because we live in an "instant" culture. But taking the time for healing places us in a position for God to show us the source of our injury and make the needed corrections. It also allows God to gently remove the scars.

Professional trainers know it takes time for injuries to heal. The more diligent we are to apply the doctor's prescription and go through the proper rehabilitation, the quicker we recover. Yet it still takes time. Charles Austin became a champion because he believed correctly and acted wisely—and in the right time he won the Olympic gold.

When you and I appropriate God's grace by faith and then train on the straight path, we will one day receive the gold. The Atlanta Olympics won't compare to that day. Oh, what a day that will be!

1. Charles Austin, *Head Games: Life's Greatest Challenge* (Austin, Texas: TurnKey Press, 2007) 81.

2. Ibid., 66.

3. Ibid.

4. Ibid., 66–67.

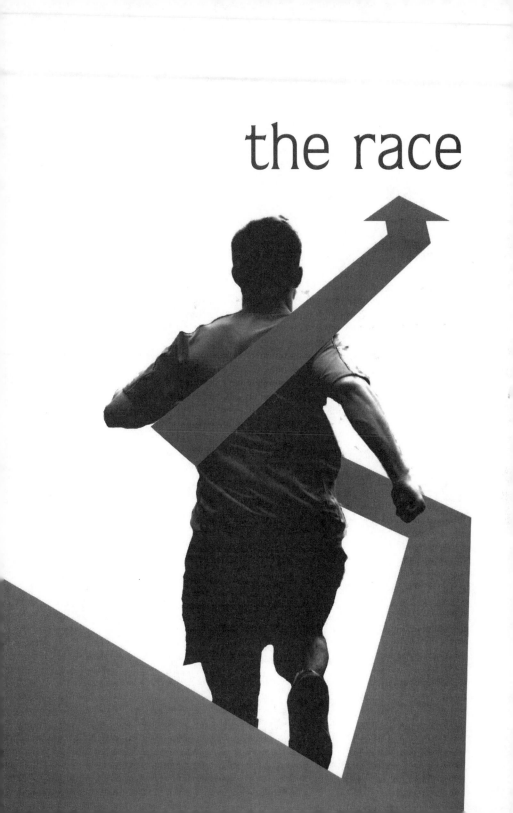

the race

running with endurance

There's something about community and unity—doing something with 40,000 other people who are all running the same race that I'm running, with the same goals, getting to that finish line.
Ryan Hall

Do you not know that all the runners in a stadium compete, but only one receives the prize? So run to win. Each competitor must exercise self-control in everything. They do it to receive a perishable crown, but we an imperishable one.
1 Corinthians 9:24–25

The renewal in my personal life began with a cancer diagnosis and a call to run, but the ultimate challenge came the day I ran the Athens Classic Marathon. I learned much from training but even more from the race. Running 26.2 miles carried plenty of challenges, but I've discovered over the past forty years that God's call always holds surprises. The Athens Classic Marathon was no different.

Tex and I traveled to Europe more than a week before the marathon. I ministered in Holland among Iranians who live in Western Europe, then conducted a leadership training seminar with Greek pastors and leaders just outside Athens. Two days prior to the race, I joined an American running tour group in Athens.

Tex started feeling ill the last day of the leadership seminar. Kirsta Leeburg Melton (the daughter of my friend Ken who had been killed in an auto accident) and her husband Wade joined Tex and me at the hotel where the American running group stayed. There was a "carbo loading" pasta dinner for the runners the night before the race. Tex felt sick during the meal and excused herself, returning to our room. Kirsta, Wade, and I visited with many of the runners, trying to get an idea of what to expect. It was our first attempt at 26.2 miles, but almost everyone else was a seasoned marathoner. Some were running as much as one marathon per month. Others had run fifteen to twenty-five marathons.

Kirsta shared her story with other runners, who were deeply moved. She told them about her dad's dream to run the Athens Classic Marathon and that when she learned I was training to complete the dream, she knew she had to run in his place. She came to Athens with his dream, his photo, and even his name on her bib.

A couple runners asked me about my goals. I told my story about the cancer and how I felt called to run. Then I said, "First, I want to finish. It's my first marathon. Then, I would like to qualify for Boston."

They looked at me as though I had just said the most stupid thing they had ever heard. They were probably right—not about finishing, but about Boston.

"This is not the race to qualify for Boston," one runner said. "The hills will kill you. I know a flat marathon that will give you a better chance." He was right, but the dream was to run the original marathon course. And, hey, I'm a dreamer.

I returned to our room to get to bed early and found that Tex was feeling progressively worse. When I awoke early the morning of the race, Tex was running a fever. I told her we must find a doctor—and I held her as she cried.

"Your health is important," I whispered. "We've got to get you well. I'm going to the front desk and see if they can call a doctor."

The hotel was great. They contacted a doctor who immediately came to see Tex. Meanwhile I tried to get my gear together for the race. In the midst of everything, I forgot the nutritional gel I was planning to carry. The doctor gave Tex some medication, but it didn't kick in before I had to leave. I didn't expect the race to begin like this.

TO THE STARTING LINE

The Athens Classic Marathon could be called the mother of all marathons. When Kirsta and I boarded the bus at the original Olympic stadium in Athens to travel to the starting line in the village of Marathon, a mixture of adventure, dread, fear, and excitement filled our hearts.

Kirsta looked out the window and waved goodbye to Wade. I took a deep breath. My heart was heavy because of Tex. She had walked with me every step of the way the past thirty years of this incredible journey to Greece. I had leaned on her many times, and she had always been there. I wanted her with me because I knew this was more than a race. I knew I was about to learn some incredible life lessons. Before I left the hotel, she cried as I held her.

"I know how important this is to you," she said. "I want to be there. We've been together in this the entire time. I want to see it completed. I want to watch you cross the finish line."

"I know, sweetheart," I said. "I love you. It will be okay. And don't worry about me. I'll make it—by God's grace. I'll complete this journey today. You just take care of yourself and do what the doctor says."

It was hard to walk out of the room and leave her with the physician. The journey had already been filled with dozens of detours. As I walked out of the hotel, I wondered, *What's going to happen next?* We both knew it was now or never. Today was the day to follow through with a thirty-year-old vision that had been birthed in the mountains of Germany. There might not be another opportunity.

Once Kirsta and I got on the bus, neither of us understood one word of what was said. We knew our fellow travelers came from around the world with one purpose: to run the same course that Pheidippides ran in 490 B.C.

As I stared out the window, emotions overwhelmed me. It had been a long journey to board that bus—three decades. During those years, three dear friends had been killed. A colleague had been murdered by terrorists. I'd gone through cancer surgery and was injured just five weeks before we left for Athens.

Now I faced the part of the journey that haunted me most: my fears. My mind raced with questions. Was I attempting this marathon too soon after my cancer surgery? Would my back injury five weeks earlier keep me from finishing?

Neither Kirsta nor I possessed a high level of confidence, but we had hearts filled with determination. Kirsta planned to complete her father's dreams no matter what. She told me she would crawl across the finish line if necessary. I believed her. As for me, the 26.2 miles would teach me lessons I could learn only as I climbed the hills leading to Athens. But I determined to learn whatever God was trying to teach me. Life had been confusing the past four years. My goal was far beyond running a marathon. I hoped the race held answers. Most of all, I hoped I had the capacity to finish.

Once we arrived at the village of Marathon, Kirsta met some American military personnel who were running. They planned to run about the same pace as she did. I left her with them and found a place a little closer to the front of the pack. Thousands of runners began shouting with the countdown. The gun went off. The race was on.

TO THE FINISH LINE

Several questions needed answering as I began the race. *What deep-seated truths were needed to complete the race? Would I finish at my full potential? What lessons would I learn about life?* I was about to discover the answer to all but one of those questions.

The longest I ran during training was twenty miles. I had planned to run twenty-two, but the back injury kept me from building my mileage to that point. But I felt fairly confident because the hills stopped at twenty miles. I thought if I could make it to the top of the hills, the rest would be downhill or flat. That would be a piece of cake. The real challenge would come as I climbed the hills—or so I thought.

I learned so much through the preparation and training stages, and my training paid off. I maintained my pace through the first twenty miles. But there were some factors I missed in my preparation. The first was psychological. I had read about mental toughness but didn't really appreciate what I studied. Somewhere between the twenty-first and twenty-second mile, I discovered the importance of a tough mental attitude.

Once I completed the hills around mile twenty, I was elated—extremely tired but very confident. I had done what my friend Ken taught me—conquered the hills. At that point I let down my guard and lost focus. I began to think, *I'm going to do this. I made it up the hills, and I'm still on pace. I'll qualify for Boston.*

The race organizers, however, had done the unexpected. A short distance after the hills, the course came to a major inter-section in Athens. I thought they would have blocked traffic so the runners could go directly through the intersection. Instead, runners were diverted through a tunnel that went under the intersection. No problem going into the tunnel. But what goes down must come up. When I began to ascend, I wasn't prepared. I lost confidence and began walking.

That's when things fell apart. As I tried to run again, every-thing began aching. It started in my hips. Pain in the left hip. Then the right one. I jogged, walked, and jogged again. I knew if I continued walking, I wouldn't qualify for Boston. The pain became worse. I hurt so badly. My only goal was to make it to the next refreshment table. I thought if I could get something to drink, I would bounce back.

I made it to the table, but there was no bouncing. Only walking slowly. The pain spread to my quads, then my calves. It was excruciating. My goal was no longer to make it to the next refreshment table, but to the next mile marker.

Once I made it there, the pain became unbearable. I then set my sights on making it to the next red light.

By the time I arrived at the light, everything ached. My feet felt like they were on fire. At that point, I whispered a prayer. "God, I don't care about Boston. Please, just help me finish." Speed was no longer important. The only thing that mattered was finishing.

I hobbled a little farther. Right before turning onto the final stretch leading to the ancient Olympic stadium, I could no longer move. I had never felt such pain. My hips. My legs. My feet. Pain roared through them like a wildfire.

I bent over—my head hanging down and tears flowing. It was over. The dream. The lessons. A year and a half of training. "Oh, God," I cried. "Please help me. Let me make it around the corner so I can at least see the stadium and the finish line."

I placed my left hand under my right hamstring and pulled my leg up and forward. I repeated the action with my right hand and left hamstring. I finally made it to the corner and turned onto the final stretch toward the stadium. At that moment, something incredible happened. My life will forever be changed.

Hundreds upon hundreds of people lined the street. They yelled, "Bravo, bravo!" Down the street, I could see the stadium filled with throngs of people. Everyone cheered the athletes as they ran toward the stadium.

I don't understand how, but I lifted my legs and jogged. Strength flowed from the cheering crowds into my exhausted legs. The farther I ran, the larger the crowds. As I entered the stadium, it was just as Ken said it would be. Thirty years earlier Ken had said, "We may not be the fastest or have the prettiest race, but we'll run on a historic path. Entering that original Olympic stadium will be overwhelming." It was.

Everything hurt as I entered the stadium, but it didn't matter. I saw the finish line—and nothing could keep me from crossing it. My entire mind and body focused on crossing the line. As I finished the race, I pointed my finger toward heaven. Immediately, race officials placed a medal around my neck.

AN ETERNAL PERSPECTIVE

When I stepped across the finish line, I learned two important truths. First, I learned the power of having an eternal view of the race. When I turned that corner and heard the cheering crowds, it seemed straight out of Hebrews 12:1—"Since we are surrounded by such a great cloud of witnesses…." The great heroes of the faith have run their race, and they're in God's grandstands watching us run. They faced the same difficulties. They encountered times of complete exhaustion in their race, but they finished—and they're pulling for us because they know a crown awaits us when we cross the finish line.

We may feel as though we can't go any farther or do any more. We may be at the end of ourselves and feel no one un-

Sammy finishes the original *Athens Classic Marathon*.

derstands. But that's not true. Multitudes have been at the same place. They know what we feel. They understand the pain—and they finished. They're cheering for us.

"Bravo! Bravo! You can do it!" reverberates from heaven's grandstands. Paul knew the crown awaited him. He wants you to remember that your race ends as eternity begins. We must not forget the eternal perspective. Multitudes are cheering for us in those heavenly grandstands.

FOCUS ON THE FINISH

A second truth also enabled me to complete the race. Once I saw the finish line, nothing could stop me. If I had needed to pull myself across the line with my arms, I would have done it. An incredible power arose the moment my eyes were fixed on the finish line. It defied my helpless state and produced power I couldn't explain.

That's why the author of Hebrews says, "Keeping our eyes fixed on Jesus, the pioneer and perfecter of our faith" (12:2). Jesus is our starting line and our finish line. If we begin anywhere else, we've started in the wrong place. We begin by looking to Jesus. We continue and conclude the race with our eyes fixed on Him.

Imagine you're in that original Olympic stadium. You stumble into the stadium but have no strength to make it to the finish line. Everything looks a blur. As you attempt to focus, you recognize faces among the crowd. You see Abraham, the father of our faith. You recognize Moses, God's great leader. You see Paul, the apostle and church planter. A host from history is gathered in the stadium watching as you stumble, almost ready to collapse.

A hush falls on the throng. Abraham lifts his voice. Like thunder roaring through the stadium, his words fall on everyone: "Look to Jesus."

More silence.

Then Moses speaks. "Look to Jesus."

Next Paul. "Look to Jesus."

The crowd chants in unison, "Look to Jesus. Look to Jesus. Look to Jesus."

You lift your head and direct your eyes toward the finish line. You see Jesus waiting with a crown of life. You fix your eyes on Him—and strength flows from the soles of your feet to the top of your head. Your arms move. Then your legs. You run. You finish the race and collapse in the arms of Jesus and hear the words, "Well done."

finishing well

"This race, instead of pushing myself, I felt like God was pulling me," [Wesley] Korir said. "I kept thinking those runners would sprint to pass me up. I just kept running." When he crossed the finish line in two hours, eight minutes, 24 seconds, Korir dropped to his knees, a full minute ahead of the second place finisher. He broke his own record, slashing five minutes, 27 seconds off his personal best time. "All I was thinking was 'thank you Jesus'" he said. [1]

"Wesley's Win" in *The Southeast Outlook*

With this goal in mind, I strive toward the prize of the upward call of God in Christ Jesus.

Philippians 3:14

After I crossed the Athens Classic Marathon finish line, I collapsed and was carried to the medical tent. Later, medical personnel took me by ambulance to the hospital, where physicians helped me recover. Johnathan, who had been photographing me when I collapsed, didn't want to scare Tex by telling her what happened. So he called her a couple hours later and told her I was really tired and lying down. He didn't tell her I was resting in the medical tent! But, once the sun set, he had to tell her everything. He called and assured her I was okay but that the doctors were making sure I recovered completely. It was later that night before I made it back to the hotel.

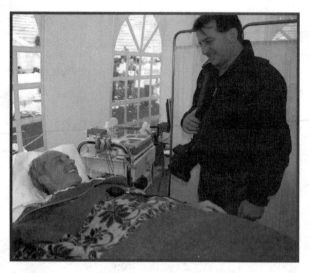

Sammy in the medical tent after finishing the *Athens Classic Marathon.*

We flew to Amsterdam the next day and then on to India, where we began ministry in the state of Punjab. On the flights I pondered what happened during the race. I had trained for more than a year, and after I completed the hills was on target to qualify for Boston. But in the end I came up short. Were my expectations too high? Did I make a mistake that kept me from qualifying? Was my training program inadequate?

Evaluation is a necessary part of the race, and I knew that if I wanted to improve I must ask the hard questions and be willing to accept the truth. That's true not only for the Athens Classic Marathon, but also for life. The psalmist said, "Examine me, and probe my thoughts! Test me, and know my concerns! See if there is any idolatrous tendency in me, and lead me in the reliable ancient path!" (Psalm 139:23–24). He wanted to know the tendencies that kept him from running his race at full potential. To pray that prayer took humility, honesty, and a willingness for the Holy Spirit to dig deep in his heart. If we're going to run at maximum potential, we must also be willing to ask—and have others ask—the hard questions. We must live with a keen sense of transparency.

Evaluation is critical to running at full potential. We saw earlier that Felix Limo evaluates his running to discover weaknesses. But the process of evaluation goes far beyond discovering inadequacies. It enables us to learn, grow, and discover areas of the Christian life we never dreamed existed. This isn't morbid introspection but rather the Holy Spirit searching the deepest part of our hearts.

The answers to my questions about the Greek Marathon seemed elusive. I did everything I knew to do to prepare and train for the race. All of it paid off as I climbed the hills. However, as I prayed and sought God's light to show me His truths, two critical principles came to the forefront.

COASTING CAN BE DANGEROUS

My system began to break down once I finished the hills. I had remained focused while climbing those difficult hills. But I lost that focus once I made it to the top. I didn't understand that going downhill produces just as much trauma to my body as running uphill does, if not more. I had prepared for the uphill struggle but thought that running downhill would be a piece of cake.

My body wasn't prepared for the drastic changes and demands of running downhill. I should have known because I have preached in South Africa numerous times, and several South African friends have run in the popular Comrades Marathon. It's an "ultra distance" fifty-six-mile race between

Pietermaritzburg and Durban. Each year, the race alternates the starting place—either Pietermaritzburg or Durban. When the race begins in Durban, the course is mostly uphill. There are five major hills the runners have to climb. But when it begins in Pietermaritzburg, the race is primarily downhill. Most of my South African runner friends tell me that running downhill is much more difficult.

But I wasn't thinking about the Comrades when I reached the top of the hills in Athens. I thought, *I'm okay now. I've made it to the top.* I didn't realize that I was facing the most challenging part.

It's that same principle in our spiritual lives that many leaders fail to recognize once they arrive at the pinnacle of their ministry. They think they can coast. They lose focus and then everything falls apart. I've known Christian leaders who truly love God yet failed once they became prominent in the Christian community. Many had risen to the top by overcoming difficulties that caused them to walk closely with God. Once they arrived in a place where they seemed comfortable in their race, however, they subtly thought they could run in their own power.

Coasting can be very deceptive. When you look at victorious Christian living in the Bible, you discover that most of our victory lies in the way we think. If we think in a biblical manner, we become winners. But when we think in self-centered ways, victory quickly turns to defeat. It takes a long time to climb a hill but only a few seconds to fall off a cliff. Be careful when coasting or going downhill. It can be dangerous.

Some of my greatest disappointments have come after the greatest victories. One of the great revivals in the history of the church took place in Romania during the revolution. What most news coverage refused to report was that the revolution began in the church, when an evangelical pastor was about to be arrested. Christians from all denominations went to his home to protect him. The dreaded *Securitate* (Secret Police) fired on innocent men, women, and children.

Tens of thousands of people gathered in the square of Timisoara to protest the tragedy. A pastor friend stood and preached, and a miracle took place. More than 100,000 atheists began shouting, "There is a God! There is a God!" This scene spread to every major population center in the country. Revival spread. Freedom descended. It was an awesome moment.

For decades Christians had struggled under communist domination. They climbed incredible hills. Then I watched in horror as a few of my friends began to "coast." For them it was now a downhill race. No more persecution. They wouldn't lose their jobs or face prison for their faith. Men who stood fearlessly in the face of persecution succumbed to the subtle temptations in a free society. They weren't prepared for the downhill part of the race, and everything fell apart in their lives. They lost focus on what gave them victory. Their fall was short, fast, and devastating.

One of the lessons I learned from the Greek Marathon was that the greatest temptations often come after we've conquered the hills. We lose focus and begin to drift from biblical truths that enabled us to overcome them. Our greatest dangers often lie at the top of the summit.

NUTRITION DURING THE RACE

When I returned from India to San Antonio, an endurance clinic was being conducted at a local running store. The seminar was led by Amanda McIntosh, who has a long list of championships in ultra-marathons including the 1999 female U.S.A. 50 Mile Trail championship, the Leadville 100, and the 2005 Women's Champion of the World Masters 100 km. I was excited to hear this champion and distance coach. I hoped I would learn more about why I hadn't run to my full potential.

I wasn't disappointed. Coach McIntosh was filled with training tips. But it was her advice on nutrition during the race that captured my thinking. "Before I speak to you about my training," she said, "I want to talk to you about nutrition *during* the race." Nutrition had been a big part of what I had learned about endurance racing. Most of it, however, had involved training. She began to talk about one of the greatest mistakes long distance runners make during a race.

She described a process called "glycogen depletion." Instead of trying to explain all the science behind the concept, McIntosh brought us quickly to the bottom line. Once you have run for three hours at race pace, your glycogen stores are nearly depleted. Those stores provide energy to your muscles. If you have not replenished your glycogen during the race or you don't have enough glycogen stored, you become fatigued and lose all energy.

After the clinic, I described to McIntosh what happened in Athens and asked if glycogen depletion was the cause. Yes, she said that likely caused my breakdown. In marathon circles, it's often called "hitting the wall." I would have described it as "the wall hitting me, then falling on me and burying me." Only by the grace of God was I resurrected from the grave of glycogen depletion!

The condition has two common cures. First, make sure that you have filled your glycogen stores before the race. That's why eating carbohydrates as you lead up to race day is important. But it is just as important to replenish your glycogen stores during the race. When I left my hotel room the morning of the race, I was concerned about Tex and forgot my gel packs. They were small packages of a carbohydrate and protein mix that my body could easily assimilate during the race to replenish my glycogen. When I boarded the bus, I realized what I had forgotten. I was a little concerned but figured it wasn't too important. I would stop at the refreshment tables and drink plenty of liquids. Those liquids definitely helped. But this one small mistake nearly un-raveled all of my training.

As I contemplated my mistake, I remembered the words of Jesus, "Man does not live by bread alone, but by every word that comes from the mouth of God" (Matthew 4:4). Successfully running the race of life demands that we regularly digest God's Word. It's critical not only during our training but also during the race. Too many of us take in God's Word for a season but fail to replenish ourselves throughout the race.

Jesus gives us a perspective on our study of the Bible when He says, "You study the scriptures thoroughly because you think in them you possess eternal life, and it is these same scriptures that testify about me" (John 5:39). People often study the Bible to receive some special assurance of eternal life, victorious life, or a healthy life. All those are good, but Jesus reminds us those aren't the purpose of the Scriptures. The Bible points us to the nature and essence of God and describes Jesus as the exact representation of God. It shows us Jesus. If we're to run the race and not become exhausted, we must take His Word into the deepest part of our hearts.

We must partake of His Word in a way that enables us to digest it easily during the race. How do we do that? Look for Jesus on every page of the Bible. It testifies of Him. It shows us His nature and character. As we see Him in the Bible, we find strength, character, and endurance to run the race He has given us. We need daily to see Jesus and ask God to make us more like Him. There is so much to His character and deeds. It takes a lifetime to discover the wonder, beauty, and splendor of Jesus. So we must consistently and devotionally read the Scriptures. Strength and endurance flow from seeing Him.

God's Word in Romans 8:29 clearly states our purpose: God "predestined [us] to be conformed to the image of his Son." God has a destiny for all of us: conformity to the image of Jesus. That's the finish line. It's the place we're running toward. It's the purpose of our race. Holiness. Conformity to the image of Jesus. Loving God and loving people.

God's Spirit prepares us as we wait on Him, and then He leads us on paths that conform us to the image of Jesus. He strips away everything that doesn't resemble Jesus and teaches us how to live as winners. Hills, difficulties, weaknesses—none of them can keep us from victory as long as our eyes are focused on Jesus.

We run at our greatest potential when we see Him—the One True Champion of life, the One Who loved those who hated Him, the One Who cared for those despised by others, the One Who helped the hurting, the One Who befriended the lonely, the One Who shattered the darkness, the One Who conquered death. The purpose of our race isn't to make us bigger, better, or more well known. His purpose for us is found in His likeness. His purpose takes us down a road of conformity into His image. It's the path we pursue, the race we run.

When we run down this road, our final cry will be, "Nenikékamen!" Rejoice, we conquer!

---

1. "Wesley's Win," *The Southeast Outlook*, June 4, 2009, 13.

appendix

interview with ryan hall

One of the great U.S. long distance runners, Ryan Hall, on January 4, 2007, became the first American to run a half marathon under one hour. His titles include 2008 Olympic Trials Men's Marathon champion, 2007 U.S. Half Marathon champion, 2006 U.S.A. Cross Country champion, and 2005 NCAA 5,000 Meter champion.

Sammy: Why do you run?

Ryan: My wife and I love to ask other people that. When I started out on my very first run, I did it around Big Bear Lake when I was 13 years old. I felt like God told me that He had given me a gift, and that gift is to be used to help other people. So I run to accomplish that. And, in pursuing that, I find fullness of life and fullness of joy—which is what I think we're all looking for. I feel like I've accomplished the mission that God has given me, and I'll continue to go down this running path that I have been on for the last 13 years.

Sammy: What are your running goals?

Ryan: I've gone back and forth with having very tangible running goals to having more philosophical goals as

I've gotten older. I used to write down the times I wanted to run. At one point, before the 2004 Olympics, I was very obsessive about wanting to be at the Olympics and run well in them. I even had a countdown on my wall in my college dorm that started 1000 days out—counting down every single day. I realized that it was too intense, and I was getting too obsessive. I was making everything, my whole life, just about one day—trying to qualify or go to the Olympics. I realized that wasn't a healthy way to look at life, and that I was missing a lot of life in the meantime. Now, my main goals are more philosophical. Before I ran Boston, it was just to run with freedom and joy. Often, I'll have these key words that God has given me for certain races that I want to experience in my heart. Then, obviously, there are some things that I'd love to accomplish before I'm done. But I look at those as secondary goals. Obviously, things like winning the Boston Marathon one day, that's a big goal of mine. I'd love to break the American or world record in a marathon at one point. That would be really fun. But, I look at those—if they happen, that's great. But, if not, I know that I can live without them.

Sammy: You talked about Boston in one of your blogs and made this statement: "My hamstrings were on fire. Everything hurt but I tried to enjoy the moment as best as I could despite the pain. Running has taught me how to enjoy even the not so pleasant moments." For most people joy and pain are a contradiction. Can you explain what you meant by joy in the midst of pain?

Ryan: It's a hard thing to describe. When I think about joy in midst of the pain, I think of Jesus going to the cross for the joy set before Him. It's not that that moment feels particularly good, but knowing that you're going after something, and that you're devoting your whole heart to it. You're pushing yourself, and you're going after the mission that God has put you on. And out of that flows joy. It's definitely not that there's a lot of joy in the actual sensation of pain, but there's a definite joy in your heart, when you feel, "Okay, I'm going after this. I'm giving it everything I have." There is a ton of joy that comes as a result of that.

Sammy: Is there anything you can do to develop a spirit of joy? When you know you're facing pain, is there anything you can do, practically, philosophically, or spiritually to develop that attitude?

Ryan: Absolutely. One of my favorite verses in the Bible is in Psalms. It says, "In His presence there's fullness of joy" (Psalm 16:11). That verse gets me every time I think about it. It's so true. When you're in His presence, there's so much joy. What I pray when I'm out there racing and going through those hard times is just to be in the presence of God. I want to find a way to connect with Him in those hard moments because whenever I'm in His presence I always feel the joy. I think that's the best way to find joy—just to connect and to be in His presence.

Sammy: In college you ran the mile. What caused you to think that your race was going to be the marathon rather than the mile? What produced that change?

Ryan: It took me a long time to be open to that change because I was so fixed on the mile as I was growing up. I was so into it. I wasn't about to let anyone tell me that I couldn't do the mile, that I couldn't be the best miler in the world. That was my goal for myself. And it took a lot to finally bring me down to what God had for my running in terms of picking out an event. It came after a lot of heartbreak. I had a lot of bad races in college—came in last place race after race. I wasn't improving at all, and it was just a frustrating time. But that made me open up my hand to the gift that God gave me. I thought, "All right Lord, I don't care what event You want me to do. I just want to do what You've created me to do." And when I came to that point, I was starting to experiment with the longer races and it came very natural to me. Afterwards, now looking back, I'm thinking, "Man, I wish I would've gotten wise to that faster."

Early on, you would have thought after my first run, which was 15 miles, that I would've known that I was made to run longer, but it took me almost 10 years to figure it out.

Sammy: For the marathon or any long distance, what's been the most helpful training concept you've had?

Ryan: One of the biggest things is letting it come to you and not forcing things to happen. When you want something really bad, it's easy to try really hard. The Bible says, "Cease striving and know that I am God" (Psalm 46:10 NASB). Sometimes, we want God so much. We try so hard. We discipline ourselves, and we try to force God to show up. But sometimes there are setbacks. We need to learn to enjoy His presence, not try to force it to happen. It's not that we shouldn't try and connect with God because we definitely should spend time doing that. But having the mindset of freedom, just letting it come naturally, and it's the same thing in training. Whenever I'm "putting the pedal to the metal" every day in practice, running my guts out in workouts, and just trying to go after it, it seems like it doesn't go so well. But those times when I'm just out there having a good time, enjoying myself, open to whatever outcome, and trusting God with my training and racing, things seem to click a lot better.

Sammy: You mentioned in a blog that when you ran Boston, the crowd support was amazing. How important is it to have a support group, a team around you, and then the general support? What role does that play in enabling you to achieve your greatest potential?

Ryan: It's huge having a support crew and having people out on the race course supporting me. You can run a marathon any day you want to in practice. What makes it special is sharing that with other people, sharing the experience with other guys you're running with, with the crowd, and that's when you're able to test what's inside of you and push yourself to levels that you didn't even think possible. But you can't do it on your own. There's something about community and unity—doing something with 40,000 other people who are all running the same race that I'm running, with the same goals, getting to that finish line. In terms of surrounding myself with supportive people, that is huge. Having my wife around me day in and day out and having her encouragement is huge. Being able to talk to her about what's on my heart, whether it's bad workouts or good workouts, or things I'm thinking about or what God's speaking to me about—it's just huge. Also, I try to glean from as many people as I can and learn as much as I can from my coach, teammates, therapists, and nutritionists. I try to surround myself with lots of wise counsel. And I think that's so important in training.

Sammy: What does running competitively do for you that is different from just going out and enjoying a nice run? What does the competition do for you as a person?

Ryan: I've spent a lot of time thinking about competition, and what you should get out of the whole experience. If Jesus had my profession, how would He do it? What would His heart be like? As I thought about that, I know that Jesus would be able to push Himself harder than anyone out there, and He would do some amazing things, even without having to tap into His divinity. If He did it purely through the man side of Him, I think that we would've seen an amazing runner who could push Himself to levels that we wouldn't ever think possible because of the spiritual and physical connection. I feel like they're so intertwined—the spirit, the emotion, and the body. The more able you are to be a complete person, the better athlete you're going to be and the better person you're going to be.

With that said, I've thought about what His motivation and His heart would be like while He's out there running. I don't think He would be looking to the person next to Him thinking, "Oh, I really want to beat this person," or "I really want to win this race so I can receive all this glory and fame." There are lots of verses in the Bible that talk about not comparing yourself to others. My favorite comes from the end of John where Jesus died, comes back, and is talking to Peter.... Then Peter asks Him, "Well what about him?" pointing to John. And He basically said, "If I want him to stay until I return again, what's that to you? But you follow Me." It's about not comparing yourself to others. [Comparing] what God has for other people is a huge thing to avoid when it comes to competition. But there should be something that pushes us where we're very eager to lay down our bodies as sacrifices to the Lord. And also, there's so many physical lessons that you can learn that apply to the spiritual—through training, discipline, and hard work and going through painful moments out there on the road. But I think Jesus would've pushed Himself to accomplish the goal that God had set for Him in His running. So I strive to have those same things pushing me to do better than I otherwise could. I want to see some of the guys that I'm running next to as guys that Jesus loves, whom I love. We help each other get to new levels.

Sammy: The Kenyan runners have achieved so much. What do you think? Is it because of genetics, training, nutrition, or motivation? Do you have any idea why they're doing so well? Can Americans compete with them?

Ryan: I think it's a combination of all those things that you've thrown out. For one thing, their country is really into it. Why aren't the Kenyans great at baseball, basketball, football, swimming, or cycling? They are not such a big deal in their country, but running has become the big deal there. It's easily accessible. Everyone can do it. Kids grow up being inspired by these elite runners who can do amazing things. It creates a lot of interest and gets a lot of talent out there. They have a big pool of kids to draw from, and they are running a ton of mileage at a very young age. I think one of the biggest things is that in their culture it's seen as something fun. My wife and I went to Zambia in 2008 with World Vision to check out some of the projects funded in Zambia. We'd be out running, and the kids would start running with us. The little girls running home from school in the woods and everything—they're smiling, laughing, and just having the best time. In our culture, being active is not so much fun for kids. They have so many other things that entertain them, and running is not often one of them. It's certainly not one of the major sports in the U.S. It's not getting the same attention that baseball, basketball, and football have gotten. So it has less of a draw for kids. They don't see it as fun. Whenever you're not having fun doing something, and it's used as punishment, I don't think you're going to see as good of results.

I think those are some of the contributing things. Obviously, the things you're talking about are important, like eating really well. Their nutrition is good. It's simple, straightforward. Also, they have a body type that seems to be made to run. So I think it's cool in a lot of ways that they're as successful as they are. Here we are, a developed U.S., with so many things that are at our hands in terms of science and nutrition. We have so much opportunity here, and yet people who are the poorest of the poor are dominating the sport, at least right now.

We're starting to see U.S. guys getting up there and competing with them. And I think a big part of it is believing that we can. I know a lot of guys in the past have gone to the starting line, already defeated when they see the Kenyan guys. They're thinking, *He's going to beat me.* But that's starting to change as guys are starting to run with them more and be more competitive at their level. If we can continue to show them at events like the major marathons and track meets that we can compete with these guys, more kids are going to start believing and go after it.

Sammy: You mention in one of your blogs that you wanted to prepare your heart for the race. What did you mean by that, and how does a person prepare their heart to run a race?

Ryan: I tell myself that over and over. I've spent so much time training my physical body, but I'm constantly telling myself the most important thing I can train is my heart. And I really believe it's the heart that drives the body. And it's the heart that enables us to endure whatever's thrown at us—whether it's a good race or a bad race, or a good buildup or bad buildup. It's really the determining factor in life. The Bible says, "Above all else guard your heart for in it are the wellsprings of life" (Proverbs 4:23). That's so true. So, I try to spend a lot of time dealing with the emotions that I feel. I try to identify why I'm feeling a certain way, and it's a long process. I certainly don't have it figured out. But I'm moving in the direction where I know we can compete with the same heart that Jesus competes with and be driven by the same things that drive Him. That's what I'm after because I believe it's the freedom that Jesus came to give in all areas of life. It can be a beautiful thing if we can get there. That's what drives and motivates me to get my heart totally pure. I think about those things when I'm not running, and it doesn't happen overnight. I try to spend time praying, in God's Word, and being transformed in those ways and then let God do the work. With the heart, it requires a lot of prayer. God has to move to change your heart in so many ways. So, I just pray for that a lot.

Sammy: What's the greatest struggle that you've faced while running or as an athlete?

Ryan: I think the biggest struggle is one of pride because it creeps up in so many different ways. It's not that

I'm thinking, *Oh, I'm the bomb. I had this great race or whatever. I'm so awesome.* I've gotten past thinking lots of those thoughts, but it manifests itself in so many different ways. It shows up in how you might treat someone better because they're a better runner than another guy on your team, and you wonder, *Why do I treat him that way and I don't give this other guy the time of day because he's not as fast?* It just shows up in so many different ways that it is one that I continually work on. And I'm so inspired by Moses, the most humble man to walk the earth. I want to walk in his steps.

Sammy: You ran in the Olympic trials in New York and won. Then you learned, shortly thereafter, that your colleague and friend, Ryan Shay, had collapsed and died during the race. How did you deal with that? I know that your wife was close to his wife, and that must've been traumatic for the two of you. What did you do to be able to look at that and to keep going?

Ryan: It was tough. The Lord told us that we should weep with those who weep and rejoice with those who rejoice. We celebrated my victory that night, but then we were also with Alicia, and we were mourning the loss of a friend. It was a tough day. Emotions were just all over the place. In the end, we just knew that God's a good God, and we have to continually put our trust in Him—that He knows what's best for us.

I don't necessarily believe I know the whole purpose behind what happened. It seems way too random to have Ryan pass out and pass away in the Olympic trials for the marathon. It just seems way too coincidental, and I don't know where my theology necessarily stands on that. Was it God or was it the Devil or was it just natural? Sometimes I think you just have to be okay with not knowing, and you have to trust that God is good. You just have to put your trust in Him.

Sammy: Have you ever been injured before an important race?

Ryan: I've had injuries that took me out of the Olympic trials in 2004. I've had stuff like that happen. I've actually had really good fortune with the marathons. In all of my major marathons, I've gone to the starting line healthy and in shape. But certainly, in 2004 I had a hamstring injury that cut me out of the trials, and that was definitely difficult.

Sammy: Is there anything you can do to prevent injury or to overcome injury prior to races that you would encourage people to do?

Ryan: Most injuries happen as a result of doing something new that you haven't done before. For example, a lot of injuries take place when you're just getting into running or after you've taken a break and you're just

starting back up. It happens because you're introducing a whole bunch of different stimuli that the body's
not used to dealing with. I think if you can keep
things as consistent as possible the month before the
marathon, it helps a lot. We stay with the same program. We don't take a lot of days off, keep doing the
same thing we've been doing all year. That seems to
be an effective way to stay healthy and feeling good
in those last couple months.

Sammy: Two critical factors are nutrition and hydration. Do
you have any suggestions about those?

Ryan: Those two things go hand in hand. I've learned a lot
recently by working with a nutritionist, Dr. Clyde
Wilson. He is a teacher at Stanford where I went to
school, and he's helped me a lot. Hydration's huge
in terms of being the number one thing to help you
digest your food. For example, I was having lots
of stomach problems, and it's a marathoner's worst
nightmare. If you have stomach problems in the
middle of your race, you can have a very long and
ugly day. Giving your body enough water to process
the food that you're taking in is important, especially
if you're carbo-loading those last couple days and
your body needs to process everything. It's important that it is not still in your gut when you're going
to the starting line. Drinking eight ounces of water
before and after your meals has been huge for me in

terms of processing the food. Also, having twenty ounces of water right when I get up in the morning is a great way to start out the day. I make sure that I start out hydrated. The thing that everyone wonders about is the whole carbo-load thing—whether you should do it, and how much you need. What I found is most effective for me (this is from my nutritionist) is spreading out the carbo-load over a period of two days so you're not eating an insane amount of pasta the night before the race. Your body is able to absorb it much better that way. Those things are effective in helping me to be ready at the starting line.

Sammy: You have a foundation to help eliminate poverty. Tell us why that's important to you.

Ryan: It's huge. I felt like God had given me a vision to run with the best runners in the world, but also to help other people. And, it wasn't until 2008 when I went to Zambia and saw how we could change the world, help other people, and love other people through running. Then, I became excited about starting our own foundation. I took a broader look at poverty and how we can eliminate it. As Christians, we're commanded to feed the poor and meet their needs. We saw Jesus doing that over and over and over again. That's a huge reason why I run. It took a while for us to see how we could do that. We want to, with our foundation, give other runners the opportunity to get involved and be able to love the poor through their running. So that's what we're doing. We had twenty runners at the Boston Marathon raising money for projects that we're working on, and we're having an even bigger team in Chicago this year.

So, that's been a huge way that I'm starting to see the bigger picture that running can be more than just going after your own goals. What makes it special is sharing with other people. What makes it even more special than that is being able to love other people and change other people's lives through it. I'll never forget going to Zambia and talking to a dad in the village where we had just installed a well with World Vision. He was saying, "Now that we have this clean water, I'm able to live ten years longer than I otherwise would have. My kids can grow up with clean water." It happened because a group of people ran a marathon and asked their buddies for sponsorships. That's pretty amazing stuff, and people can get up in the morning and head out the door knowing that "I'm doing something healthy, tending to my body, and training with people for a fun goal." It's an amazing experience, but ultimately it's going to make someone's life ten years longer than it otherwise would be. That is a pretty incredible thing to say you've contributed to.